CONVERSATIONS
WITH LEADERS

Books Published by the Honor Society of Nursing, Sigma Theta Tau International

Conversations with Leaders: Frank Talk from Nurses (and Others) on the Front Lines of Leadership, Hansen-Turton, Sherman, Ferguson, 2007.

Pivotal Moments in Nursing: Leaders Who Changed the Path of a Profession, Houser and Player, 2004 (Volume I) and 2007 (Volume II).

Shared Legacy, Shared Vision: The W. K. Kellogg Foundation and the Nursing Profession, Lynaugh, Smith, Grace, Sena, de Villalobos, and Hlalele. (March 2007).

Daily Miracles: Stories and Practices of Humanity and Excellence in Health Care, Briskin and Boller, 2006.

A Daybook for Nurse Leaders and Mentors. Sigma Theta Tau International, 2006.

When Parents Say No: Religious and Cultural Influences on Pediatric Healthcare Treatment, Linnard-Palmer, 2006.

Healthy Places, Healthy People: A Handbook for Culturally Competent Community Nursing Practice, Dreher, Shapiro, and Asselin, 2006.

The HeART of Nursing: Expressions of Creative Art in Nursing, Second Edition, Wendler, 2005.

Reflecting on 30 Years of Nursing Leadership: 1975-2005, Donley, 2005

nurseAdvance Collection. (Topic-specific collections of honor society published journal articles.) Topics are: Cardiovascular Nursing; Cultural Diversity in Nursing; Disaster, Trauma, and Emergency Nursing; Ethical and Legal Issues in Nursing; Genomics in Nursing and Healthcare; Gerontological Nursing; Health Promotion in Nursing; Implementing Evidence-Based Nursing; Leadership and Mentoring in Nursing; Maternal Health Nursing; Oncology Nursing; Pain Management in Nursing; Pediatric Nursing; Psychiatric-Mental Health Nursing; Public, Environmental, and Community Health Nursing; and Women's Health Nursing; 2006.

Technological Competency as Caring in Nursing, Locsin, 2005.

Making a Difference: Stories from the Point of Care, Volume I, Hudacek, 2005.

A Daybook for Nurses: Making a Difference Each Day, Hudacek, 2004.

Making a Difference: Stories from the Point of Care, Volume II, Hudacek, 2004.

Building and Managing a Career in Nursing: Strategies for Advancing Your Career, Miller, 2003.

Collaboration for the Promotion of Nursing, Briggs, Merk, and Mitchell, 2003.

Ordinary People, Extraordinary Lives: The Stories of Nurses, Smeltzer and Vlasses, 2003.

Stories of Family Caregiving: Reconsideration of Theory, Literature, and Life, Poirier and Ayres, 2002.

As We See Ourselves: Jewish Women in Nursing, Benson, 2001.

Cadet Nurse Stories: The Call for and Response of Women During World War II, Perry and Robinson, 2001.

Creating Responsive Solutions to Healthcare Change, McCullough, 2001.

Nurses' Moral Practice: Investing and Discounting Self, Kelly, 2000.

Nursing and Philanthropy: An Energizing Metaphor for the 21st Century, McBride, 2000.

Gerontological Nursing Issues for the 21st Century, Gueldner and Poon, 1999.

The Adventurous Years: Leaders in Action 1973-1999, Henderson, 1998.

Immigrant Women and Their Health: An Olive Paper, Ibrahim Meleis, Lipson, Muecke and Smith, 1998.

The Neuman Systems Model and Nursing Education: Teaching Strategies and Outcomes, Lowry, 1998.

The Image Editors: Mind, Spirit, and Voice, Hamilton, 1997.

The Language of Nursing Theory and Metatheory, King and Fawcett, 1997.

Virginia Avenel Henderson: Signature for Nursing, Hermann, 1997.

For more information and to order these books from the Honor Society of Nursing, Sigma Theta Tau International, visit the society's Web site at **www.nursingsociety.org**, or go to **www.nursingknowledge.org/stti/books,** the Web site of Nursing Knowledge International, the honor society's sales and distribution division, or call 1.888.NKI.4.YOU (U.S. and Canada) or +1.317.634.8171 (Outside U.S. and Canada).

CONVERSATIONS
WITH LEADERS

Frank Talk From Nurses (and Others)
on the Front Lines of Leadership

Tine Hansen-Turton

Susan Sherman   Vernice Ferguson

Sigma Theta Tau International
Honor Society of Nursing®

Sigma Theta Tau International

Editor-in-Chief: Jeff Burnham
Acquisitions Editor: Fay L. Bower, DNSc, FAAN
Development Editor: Carla Hall
Copy Editor: Linda Puffer

Cover Design by: Rebecca Harmon
Interior Design and Page Composition by: Rebecca Harmon

Printed in the United States of America
Printing and Binding by Printing Partners, Indianapolis, IN.

Copyright © 2007 by Sigma Theta Tau International

Sigma Theta Tau International
550 West North Street
Indianapolis, IN 46202

Visit our Web site at **www.nursingknowledge.org/STTI/books** for more information on our books.

ISBN-13: 978-1-930538-69-6
ISBN-10: 1-930538-69-3

Library of Congress Cataloging-in-Publication Data

Conversations with leaders : frank talk from nurses (and others) on the frontlines of leadership / edited by Tine Hansen-Turton, Susan Sherman, Vernice Ferguson.
    p. ; cm.
 Includes bibliographical references and index.
 ISBN-13: 978-1-930538-69-6
 ISBN-10: 1-930538-69-3
 1. Nurses—United States—Biography. 2. Nurse administrators—United States—Biography. I. Hansen-Turton, Tine. II. Sherman, Susan, 1945- III. Ferguson, Vernice. IV. Sigma Theta Tau International.
 [DNLM: 1. Nursing—Personal Narratives. 2. Leadership—Personal Narratives. 3. Nurse Administrators—Personal Narratives. WY 16 C7664 2007]

RT34.C67 2007
610.73092'2—dc22

               2007022692

First Printing – June 2007

DEDICATION

For the women and men who contributed to our inspirational conversations. Also, to Ted Wamer for his unwavering leadership and dedication to nurses.

ABOUT THE AUTHORS

TINE HANSEN-TURTON, BA, MGA, JD

Tine Hansen-Turton has more than 10 years of experience in executive management and has led the National Nursing Centers Consortium (NNCC) for the past decade. NNCC is an association of more than 190 nurse-managed health centers in the U.S. that provide quality primary health care services to one million vulnerable families annually. The mission of the association is to serve health center members by enhancing their potential for sustainability, and ensuring their growth through fostering greater recognition of them and offering services that enhance their management capabilities and programs. Tine assists organizations in developing and setting up nurse practitioner-run centers; provides technical assistance in the areas of fundraising and program development, policy development, health education, advocacy, program planning, and health center management; conducts health policy research and outcome evaluation; establishes quality care indicators for nurse practitioner care; represents nurse-managed and nurse practitioner-run health centers at local, state, and national executive and legislative branch levels; gives regular public health testimonies; and provides marketing and public relations.

Tine's accomplishments include establishing an integrated service delivery system (IDS) of nurse practitioner providers; ensuring that advanced practice registered nurses and physician assistants were defined as primary care providers in the Pennsylvania Patient's Bill of Rights Act—Act 68; negotiating changes in managed care reimbursement policies for nurse practitioners and physician assistants; ensuring that nurse practitioners received prescriptive privileges in many states; developing and implementing various nationally recognized health promotion and primary prevention programs in the health centers; and securing over $30 million dollars in direct support to nurse-managed centers.

Tine also serves as vice president for health care access and policy for Philadelphia Health Management Corporation (PHMC). In this capacity, she oversees and provides executive management services to two PHMC affiliates, the Convenient Care Association, and the Health Promotion Council.

Tine publishes in many peer-reviewed professional journals and is a regular presenter at local, state, and national healthcare conferences. She is co-author of the AJN Book of the Year Award-winning *Community and Nurse-Managed Health Centers: Getting them Started and Keeping them Going,* published by Springer Publishing Company. As a recent Eisenhower Fellow, she traveled to New Zealand and was instrumental in starting a new nurse practitioner movement and getting prescriptive authority for all nurse practitioners there. She also received the 2005 Philadelphia Business Journal Leadership Award.

Tine received her BA from Slippery Rock University, her master's in government administration from the University of Pennsylvania Fels Institute, and her juris doctor from Temple University's Beasley School of Law.

Susan Sherman, RN, MA

Susan Sherman has served as president and CEO of the Independence Foundation since 1996. The Independence Foundation, a private philanthropy with annual giving of more than $8 million, is dedicated to supporting programs in Philadelphia and the surrounding Pennsylvania counties that provide services to people who ordinarily do not have access to them. The four specific areas of funding are: Culture & Arts, Health & Human Services, Nurse-Managed Primary Health Care, and Public Interest Legal Aid.

Susan is a member of the Board of Directors of the Philadelphia Zoological Society, the Greater Philadelphia Cultural Alliance, the Greater Philadelphia Chamber of Commerce, the Philadelphia Health Management Corporation, the Advisory Committees of the Metropolitan Aids Neighborhood Nutrition Alliance Inc., Commonwealth of PA Cost Containment of Health Care and Health Care Insurance Advisory Panel, and the Mayor's Children's Commission. She is a Fellow of The College of Physicians of Philadelphia. Susan previously served as a member of the National Advisory Committee of the Robert Wood Johnson Foundation's Colleagues in Caring Project, chairperson of the Council of Associate Degree Nursing Programs, and a board member of The National League for Nursing.

Susan has been the recipient of Philadelphia Health Management Corporation's Carl Moore Leadership Awards, Community College of Philadelphia's 40 Leaders Award, MANNA's Outstanding Community Leadership Award, the Womens Way of Philadelphia: Moving Women Forward Award, The Pennsylvania Legal Services Excellence Award, the New York University School of Nursing Alumni Award, the American Academy of Nursing Civitas Award, and the Ross Laboratories Institutional Long Term Care Award. She is a member of the Pennsylvania Womens Forum, the Sunday Breakfast Club, Delaware Valley Grantmakers, and Grantmakers in Health.

VERNICE FERGUSON, RN, MA, FAAN, FRCN

Vernice Ferguson was a senior fellow in the School of Nursing at the University of Pennsylvania holding the Fagin Family Chair in Cultural Diversity. For more than 20 years, she served as a top nurse executive in federal service and was the chief nurse at two VA medical centers affiliated with academic health science centers in Madison, Wisconsin, and Chicago, Illinois. For 12 years, she was the nurse leader for the Department of Veterans Affairs, the largest organized nursing service in the world with more than 60,000 nursing personnel. Prior to the VA assignment, she served as chief of the Nursing Department of the Clinical Center, the National Institutes of Health. Ferguson is an honorary fellow of the Royal College of Nursing of the United Kingdom, the second American nurse so honored, following the late Virginia Henderson, and is a fellow and past president of the American Academy of Nursing. She is a past president of Sigma Theta Tau International, nursing's international honor society, and served as the chair of the Friends of the Virginia Henderson Library Advisory Committee. She is a past president of the International Society of Nurses in Cancer Care. Her awards and honors are numerous, including eight honorary doctorates. She was the recipient of two fellowships, one in physics at the University of Maryland and the other in alcohol studies at Yale University, and was a scholar-in-residence at the Catholic University of America. She was the Potter-Brinton Distinguished Professor for 1994 at the School of Nursing, the University of Missouri at Columbia. In 1995, she spent nine weeks in South Africa serving as visiting associate professor in the Department of Nursing Science at the University of the North West. While in South Africa in her capacity as president of the International Society of Nurses in Cancer Care, she toured the country extensively, meeting with healthcare providers in university nursing programs, voluntary associations, hospitals, and homes in townships and squatter camps. She conducted workshops and offered presentations in a variety of settings throughout South Africa, most of which were geared to cancer care and health policy issues. Ferguson serves on a number of boards and committees. Among them are: the Independence Foundation's Advisory Committee on the Nurse Managed

Primary Health Care Initiative, the Robert Wood Johnson Foundation Executive Nurse Fellows Advisory Committee, and the Board of Overseers, School of Nursing, the University of Pennsylvania. She is the founding chairman of the NOVA Foundation of the Nurses Organization of the Department of Veterans Affairs. At the 25th anniversary celebration of the American Academy of Nursing in 1998, she was honored as a "Living Legend," an exemplary role model whose contributions continue to make an impact on the provision of healthcare services in the United States and in all regions of the world.

TABLE OF CONTENTS

FOREWORD

Imagine, if you will, the conversation among three change agents who came together to celebrate the success of a series of presentations called "Conversations With Leaders." This series, ongoing since 1997, has brought together leaders from the health professions and selected others to engage an audience of practicing nurses in "conversations"—true discussions about leadership. So compelling were these "Conversations With Leaders" sessions that these change agents—Susan Sherman, a registered nurse and president of the Philadelphia-based Independence Foundation, Tine Hansen-Turton, executive director of the National Nursing Centers Consortium, and Vernice Ferguson, a registered nurse and member of the advisory committee to the Independence Foundation—knew these "conversations" should be made available to a larger and broader audience than the 50 or so who were fortunate enough to be in attendance. A book was suggested, and the three—prominent leaders in their own right—found themselves asking the leaders to recreate their "conversations" for print. This book is the culmination of that suggestion, a prime example of vision leading to action and outcome.

Most of the leaders invited to speak at the seminars began their session by telling the story of their professional careers, often moving between professional and personal stories. As this book will attest, stories are powerful teaching aides. Stories reach out to us, pull us in, and engage our immediate attention. They arouse our curiosity, and we allow ourselves to be led into the privacy of the heart and soul of the experiences of others. Stories have the effect of making abstract concepts real. Stories reveal strongly held memories, failures, successes, and lessons of leadership learned along the way.

Throughout the chapters that follow, various themes of leadership are repeated. Learning from experience is validated, proving that past successes—and even failures—can lead to future successes.

Clarification and validation of values is a common theme among the chapters. This goes hand in hand with the importance of understanding and knowing oneself. These leaders acknowledge commitment, responsibility, and accountability. Influential self-confidence is evident, and these leaders see themselves as leaders, act like leaders, and have the professional presence of leaders.

A prominent theme throughout emphasizes the role of mentors in the life of the authors. It is sometimes lonely at the top, but mentors from whom to learn and with whom to discuss issues and problems alleviate some of that isolation. Many speak of having utilized informal advisory groups with whom to share ideas and test solutions.

Leadership is about relationships, and many speak about connections, collaborations, partnerships, and teams. They acknowledge the necessity for good communication and interpersonal skills. Strategy, too, is important to move from vision to action to achievement. All the contributors, in one way or another, are change agents, using creativity and innovation to bring about change in their respective positions of leadership.

Nursing today, more than ever before, is challenged with the responsibility to change the healthcare delivery system as we know it, while providing high quality and safe care for patients in all settings. As we learn from the authors, it takes leadership to create positive change by persuading and motivating others to take action to achieve common goals. The lessons of leadership found within are profoundly personal and quite different from those found in ordinary textbooks. The stories and observations that follow not only validate our own inclinations but also inspire us to learn and adopt new strategies of leadership appropriate for our own workplace settings. These personal accounts of leadership also should encourage us to tell our own stories of leadership so that others may learn from and be empowered by them.

—Hon. Shirley S. Chater, RN, PhD, FAAN
Chair, National Advisory Committee,
Robert Wood Johnson Executive Nurse Fellows Program
President Emerita, Texas Woman's University
U.S. Commissioner, Social Security Administration, 1993 – 1997

INTRODUCTION

This book is the outgrowth of an ongoing program of informal "Conversations With…" leaders—predominantly women and nurses—who have distinguished themselves regionally and nationally in nursing, law, health, and human services. Speakers—nursing deans, cabinet officials, judges, foundation CEOs, community health center directors, politicians and policy-makers—have met in a congenial atmosphere with 40 to 60 nursing and healthcare professionals from the Philadelphia region. Each conversation reveals the personal story of that individual's path to leadership, including lessons learned, leadership tips, strategies, and practical tools. Each story is an inspiration to the audience.

"Conversations With…" are jointly sponsored by the Independence Foundation—a Philadelphia-based foundation supporting groups and organizations in public interest law, health and human services, culture and arts, and nurse-managed health centers—and the National Nursing Centers Consortium, an association of nurse-managed health centers. Community health policy makers and practitioners who attend the presentations represent a network of citizens committed to improving healthcare in their communities. The consortium and the foundation bring "Conversations With…" leaders to our community to inspire our individual and collective goals. The informal environment facilitates connections between speakers and audience that do not result from more formal events.

Those attending "Conversations With…"are nurse practitioners, other advanced practice nurses, and staff of the 25 nurse-managed health centers in urban and rural Southeastern Pennsylvania as well as academic nurse educators. The centers represented are among an estimated 250 such health centers in the U.S., managed by nurses in partnership with the communities they serve, delivering comprehensive primary healthcare and wellness services to over two million patients. Nurse-managed centers are critical safety-net providers, serving a primarily underserved patient population of all ages, more than half of whom are uninsured.

In a nurse-managed health center, a nurse occupies the chief management position, and the majority of care is provided by nurse practitioners and other advanced practice nurses. Nursing staff is responsible and accountable for client care and professional practice, and nurses are the primary providers seen by clients visiting the center. In nurse-managed health centers, health problems or potential health probems are not viewed in isolation, but within the context of societal, environmental, and cultural influences that have impacted the client's past and present health and can impact future health as well. Thus, healthcare includes patients, their families, and their communities. In many nurse-managed centers, mental health, gynecological, and midwifery services are integrated with primary care.

The women and men who speak at "Conversations With…" provide valuable stimulation and encouragement to the staff of Philadelphia-area centers. Now we are bringing these inspiring leaders to others. We have assembled a selection of the lessons learned from conversations held from 1999 to 2005 and created the book you now hold in your hands, *Conversations With Leaders: Frank Talk From Nurses (and Others) On the Front Lines of Leadership*. The support and encouragement of these wise leaders are now available to you. Please join us in having a "Conversation With…" some of the best leaders you will ever talk to.

I

LEADERSHIP IS ... INSPIRING

Good leadership is a conscious enterprise. All that you think, envision, decide, and do are guided at some level by what you believe a leader is and does.
—Marla Salmon

1

A Dozen (or so) Things I Think I've Learned About Leadership

Written by Marla E. Salmon, ScD, RN, FAAN

Leadership is a subject that has fascinated me since fourth grade—when I first became aware that it existed. A new student joined our class, changing the entire dynamic of the class and, ultimately, the course of the lives of several of us. Our small, rural community had never encountered anyone like Kris. The daughter of an archeologist, Kris had lived in many places that were unfamiliar to most of us and she wanted to be an ambassador when she grew up. From the moment that she arrived, until her tragic death five years later (and really well beyond), Kris was a leader who changed lives—mine among them. I often wonder if my life now as a citizen of the world, and my involvement in national leadership roles, grew out of Kris's introducing us to a world that was much bigger than we'd imagined. Her example and dreams challenged each of us to reach well beyond what we understood our grasp to be.

These thoughts that I am sharing about leadership are dedicated to the memory of my friend Kris and to those since who have inspired, informed, mentored, and held me accountable in my own development. To the extent that I have been a leader or, even more challenging, a good follower, I credit many people whose generosity made it possible. And, I can thank Kris for helping me to understand that one truly can make a lasting difference in the lives of others.

So, what have I learned about leadership? Perhaps the only abiding lesson is that one never stops learning about leadership—each context, exposure and experience has within it the possibility of many new lessons. Given this overarching lesson in leadership, I will offer the "Dozen (or so) Things I Think I've Learned About Leadership." I will take the liberty of sharing these in a conversational manner and my sole regret is that I won't benefit from hearing what you, the reader, has to say. (The opportunity to engage with those present during my "Conversation With…" session at the Independence Foundation was a real treat; the shared perspectives of a group are always more enriching than one talking to oneself.) Welcome reader, to half of a "Conversation With" me.

Lesson #1: Embrace a definition of leadership that frames what you do as a leader. Good leadership is a conscious enterprise. All that you think, envision, decide and do are guided at some level by what you believe a leader is and does. Take the time to think this through. (The old leadership exercise of writing one's own epitaph is worth doing.) For me, leadership is fundamentally about living out my commitment to "do good" and to "be of use." My definition also involves helping to create and communicate the vision of a better future in ways that bring people together and provide a context for shared and individual success. It includes the notion of partnering with others to develop resources and calls on me (and my partners) to act with courage and integrity.

This leads to **Lesson #2: Stand for something and, live it out.** When you have defined what leadership means to you, you have articulated a commitment that gives you a road map for everything you do. In my case, the notion of "doing good" has had a central focus on the health of vulnerable people. Nursing and public health have been the professional foundation through which I have focused my efforts. The choices I have made in my career and personal life have been guided by what I try to stand for. This has served as a framework for identifying and assessing opportunities throughout my career. It has guided me in how I've chosen to develop myself and hold myself accountable.

When one chooses to live out one's commitments, the notion of career development is quite different from the orderly, five-year plan that seems to be associated with an ideal of professional career development. A career based on seizing opportunities that advance one's capacity to make a difference is highly unpredictable and non-linear (and, never boring).

Lesson #3: Aim to be strategic all of the time. Lack of linearity and predictability does not, however, preclude the need to be strategic. When one is a leader, it is important to understand that both the journey and the destinations are equally important. Because one has a limited number of resources (including one's self), it is important to use these effectively. This requires thinking and planning. (You've heard this a million times already, right?) Let me put it a different way: If something is worth using a part of your life and that of others, it is worth spending the time making sure that this precious resource is not wasted. As an example, think about meetings and the years of our working lives that are spent in meetings that achieve absolutely nothing. A respectful leader will be clear about what the objectives are for each meeting, plan in advance, and evaluate the outcomes after the meeting in ways that lead to ongoing improvement of processes and outcomes. Such a leader will involve others in all phases of the process, creating an opportunity for the development of the leadership of others. Thinking and acting strategically demonstrate respect for others, thoughtful stewardship of resources, and respect for one's self as well.

Lesson 4: Cultivate reliable sources of advice and support. When I first became a senior government official, I met with a great nursing leader who had preceded me in that role. She shared a number of important insights and strategies. However, one crucial piece of advice was of the greatest use to me: "Get yourself a good *kitchen cabinet.*" Clearly, she wasn't referring to renovating my house. Rather, she advised me to find a few trusted, expert colleagues who could serve as a sounding board and consulting group for me on an ongoing basis.

The notion of having an informal consulting group is one that has stuck with me well beyond my years in government. When one is a leader, there is a risk of becoming isolated and caught up in the zeal of living out one's own commitments. This is a very dangerous and counter-productive tendency. Having trusted advisors who share your commitments—and are willing to challenge your thinking and strategy—is crucial to ongoing success as a leader. These advisors can provide important insights and support. They can also counteract what I have come to call "the committee in my head." This imaginary advisory board is made up of all those voices from my past that have shaped what I believe and how I see the world. It is crucial that leaders have "here and now" perspectives from people who are stakeholders in your success.

It is important to note here that a "kitchen cabinet" does not work if it is a one-way street. Reciprocity is extremely important in keeping these relationships fresh and positive. This means that leaders must *give as much or more than* they get from others and build relationships based on mutual development and support.

Lesson #5: Enable the visible success of others. The true success of leadership lies in the development of others. This means that one of the important jobs of leaders is to create contexts in which the contributions and successes of others are recognized and honored. It is important that leaders take the lead in celebrating the work of these individuals and their work with others. Leaders need to cultivate an attitude of "quiet" credit for their own work and loud, boisterous celebration of the work of others. This is not to say that leaders should have false humility or give undeserved recognition. Rather, leaders must not lose sight of the single most important fact of leadership: one cannot do it alone!

Lesson #6: The real answer is often not the obvious one. Leadership is fundamentally about finding solutions for problems and creating contexts within which progress can be made. This means understanding the factors that either impede or encourage progress.

Unfortunately, these factors are often masked by "easy explanations" or simplistic understandings of what is happening. In order to truly understand what is happening, leaders need to seek answers "above and below" those that come easily. To look "above," leaders must understand the macro dynamics of their situations. For senior leaders in institutions, this means understanding the political, social and economic contexts in which they operate. To look "below," leaders need to understand what those who are closest to the situation see. For example, the solutions to problems are often best created by those who grapple with them on a daily basis. In addition to "above and below" perspectives, leaders need to cultivate diversity and welcome perspectives that are fundamentally different from their own. Diversity offers a different set of lenses through which we can view problems and solutions, opening up new possibilities for all.

Lesson #7: Sort out what being a leader means to you as a person. Okay, so you want to be, or already are, a leader. Either reality has profound implications for who you are as a person. Most importantly, who you are as a person is the leader that you are or will become. Because leadership is a lifelong process, it inevitably interfaces with how one lives life and makes choices. Sorting out this interface is an ongoing challenge and often requires making difficult choices. Leadership is not something that one does alone: It profoundly affects loved ones, friendships, connections with others, and how one sees and feels about oneself. Dealing with these dimensions of life in direct, honest, and thoughtful ways is fundamentally important to development as both a person and leader. I have never found this process to be easy or much fun for it is a balancing act that requires sacrifice by all involved. I am fortunate to have a husband and children who have been very generous and supportive over the years. I simply could not have done all that I've been able to do without them. And, they have been enormously important to keeping my feet on the ground; they give me a reality that I need and love.

Another dimension of knowing who you are as a leader relates to understanding who you are as a follower. I believe that one cannot be a good leader without being a good follower. If one cannot step back or aside for other leadership to emerge, then one stands in the way of real progress. Good leaders do not try to keep others down. They do all that they can to elevate the leadership of others and promote their development. "Followership" is not something that is easily learned and must be cultivated as carefully and thoughtfully as leadership.

Lesson #8: Be fair to yourself. Being a leader often brings scrutiny and critique. Leaders are natural targets for frustration, anger, and blame. The challenge of being responsive and reasonably objective at the same time is enormous. Leaders must thoughtfully weigh input and not be defeated or destroyed by it. This means that leaders need to develop ways in which they can maintain a sense of balance and fairness in how they see themselves and in what they do. Humility and humor are great allies in this, as are friends and family who love you regardless of how bad a day you had. (Having a dog isn't a bad idea either.) It is also very important to have close working associates who are honest and will help you keep a realistic perspective on what is happening. Consider having a "coach"—someone who is sufficiently objective and skilled to help you overcome the challenges and issues you face. Leaders can grow through difficult times if they are able to keep a fair and constructive view of themselves and their leadership. If not, they will become isolated, uninformed, and unsuccessful.

Lesson #9: Understand that every organization is perfectly designed. Organizations are the mechanisms through which people get work done. They are both informal and formal. Leaders inevitably get involved with organizations and depend on them to produce results. For this reason, it is critical that leaders understand how organizations work and learn to interface with them in productive ways. There are many skills one can develop for this purpose. However, the single most important thing I've ever learned about organizations is that they are all effective in producing the results that you see. What this means is that if you want to change the outcomes of an organization, you need to analyze what is going on with the entire organization, not just its people. How organizations are structured, led, administered, their technology, the relationships among people, the relationships beyond the organization, and the organizational purposes and culture are all key to creating different organizational results. In short, organizations are perfectly designed to produce the results that they achieve. If one wishes to produce different results, one must change the organization.

Lesson #10: Stretch yourself all of the time. Effectiveness is learned through the process of facing challenges and the discovery that accrues through these experiences. This is one reason why it is very important for leaders to constantly stretch beyond what is usual and routine (nothing new comes from the *status quo*). The "stretching" that I refer to here includes challenging one's own ideas, beliefs, habits, and "comfort zone." It means opening oneself up to a world beyond what is currently known and believed, and trying on new ways of seeing and acting. It means choosing knowledge over ignorance and doing what is right rather than what is easy. These behaviors are absolutely necessary to growing and developing as a person and as a leader. However, self-development is not the only reason for moving beyond one's comfort zone. Perhaps even more important is that one cannot expect others to grow, learn, and "stretch" if one is not doing so him- or herself. In other words, it is crucial for leaders to live and model "stretching" as a way of being and leading.

Lesson #11: Study those you admire. Being a role model is only part of the "role modeling" equation involved in leadership development. The other part is actually benefiting from the lessons and role modeling of other leaders. The single best leadership education comes from observing, questioning, and learning from effective leaders. Make a point of identifying leaders that you admire and specifically noting what it is about them that makes them outstanding. Then, make a commitment to learn how your "admired leader" thinks about and enacts his or her leadership.

It helps to be systematic about how you study other leaders. Start a leadership journal. You might want to begin with analyzing your own leadership in relation to the topics I have addressed here by doing some self-assessment and exploration. Note areas that you wish to pursue in your ongoing development as a leader. Then, identify those leaders you most admire and keep an ongoing log of what you want to learn and what you observe and take away from these living "leadership textbooks."

Lesson #12: Things get easier when you do them over and over. Like everything else, practice is the secret to mastery. There are many things about leadership that are inherently difficult and, for many, frightening. Whether it is public speaking, making hard decisions, or standing alone on an important issue, all become easier with the skills and wisdom that accrue from practice. However, practice alone is not enough. Think about the development of world-class athletes. They practice their sports over the course of many years. But, they practice with the help and guidance of coaches who can help translate the lessons of practice into ongoing progress. What this means for leaders is that we should draw some comfort in knowing that hard things will become easier over time. But, we will only get better at doing hard things if we open ourselves up to learning and to the input and guidance of others. Another important dimension of this lesson is that unless you ask for difficult tasks or confront challenges, their learning value will be lost. The willingness to take on these experiences is, in itself, a form of leadership.

Lesson #13: Partnerships are critical. This is a lesson that is often discussed and seldom learned. In short, without partnerships, leadership is a futile exercise. It is simply impossible to make progress today without the collaborative work of people across institutions, sectors, and disciplines. However, partnership development and sustenance are only successful when skillfully conceived and managed. This means that leaders need to attend to developing this area of knowledge and skills and fostering it in others.

The dozen (or so) leadership lessons I've discussed are those I see as most central to my own understanding of leadership. However, there are a few other insights I've gained along the way, along with a few aphorisms that have kept me anchored at times. (Folk wisdom is right up there with common sense when it comes to leadership as an activity of daily living.)

One of the insights is that *each of us experiences defining moments*. These are the times when we see ourselves in new ways that offer us a glimpse of our capacities. Not all of these moments are positive or shine brightly on who we are as people. However, all are extremely valuable if we use them as opportunities to learn and fine-tune ourselves. When we experience these moments, we should take the time to record them and what we learned from them. A list of these could include (fill in the blanks):

I learned that I could be courageous and act out of principle when I

_____.

I learned how much of a difference I could make in my work when I

_____.

I learned I could act like a total idiot when I

_____.

I learned that I could be intolerant and bull-headed when I

_____.

I learned that I could underestimate others when I

_____.

I learned how privileged I was when I

_____.

There are probably many other defining moments that each of us experiences. Because they are defining, we should not forget their value to our own development as people and leaders.

I will end with my favorite quotations and then a poem. I see each as a collection of wisdom and reminder of perspectives that I often forget or overlook. They may speak to you or not. In some ways they are highly personal. At a minimum, they should serve as reminders that each of us needs touchstones in our lives—people, places, things, and ideas—that have special meaning and reach us when we most need that contact. Here is my little touchstone collection:

"The world is run by those who show up."
(Jerry Anderson, my husband)

"You can't go anywhere without leaving somewhere."
(Marceline Salmon, my mother)

"Courage is not being fearless. It is acting in the face of fear." (sign at the shoeshine stand in Minneapolis airport)

"Leave the campsite cleaner than you found it." (National Park Service)

"Bloom where you are planted." (unknown)

"Insanity is doing the same things over and over again and expecting different results." (Albert Einstein)

Guiding Sayings From My Early Days:

"If you're not part of the problem, you're part of the solution." (unknown)

"Freedom's just another word for nothing left to lose." (from the Janis Joplin song *Me and Bobby McGee*; lyrics by Kris Kristofferson)

"Sounds like a personal problem to me." (Jerry Anderson, my husband)

"Lighten up!" (Jerry Anderson, my husband)

"Live, love, laugh." (unknown)

Now, I return to where I started with my leadership lessons and the early inspiration that I drew from my childhood friend, Kris. Leadership is fundamentally about *being of use* to others and helping humankind make progress. To *be of use* is, in my mind, our most important work. The following poem was given to me by a nurse a number of years ago after a presentation I gave on the topic of leadership. It says more than I ever could:

To Be of Use
By Marge Piercy

The people I love the best
jump into work headfirst
without dallying in the shallows
and swim off with sure strokes almost out of sight.
They seem to become natives of that element,
the black sleek heads of seals
bouncing like half-submerged balls.

I love people who harness themselves, an ox to a heavy cart,
who pull like water buffalo, with massive patience,
who strain in the mud and the muck to move things forward,
who do what has to be done, again and again.

I want to be with people who submerge
in the task, who go into the fields to harvest
and work in a row and pass the bags along,
who are not parlor generals and field deserters
but move in a common rhythm
when the food must come in or the fire be put out.

The work of the world is common as mud.
Botched, it smears the hands, crumbles to dust.
But the thing worth doing well done
has a shape that satisfies, clean and evident.
Greek amphoras for wine or oil,
Hopi vases that held corn, are put in museums
but you know they were made to be used.
The pitcher cries for water to carry
and a person for work that is real.

From *The Art of Blessing the Day* by Marge Piercy, New York: Knopf. 1999, p. 73.

MARLA SALMON, ScD, RN, FAAN, is the dean of the Nell Hodgson Woodruff School of Nursing of Emory University and a professor of both nursing and public health. She is also founding director of the Lillian Carter Center for International Nursing in the School of Nursing. Dr. Salmon's leadership in these roles builds on a career that has been dedicated to improving the health of people through nursing and public health. Dr. Salmon joined Emory after serving as professor and graduate dean of the School of Nursing at the University of Pennsylvania, where she was responsible for both master-level and doctoral nursing programs. Prior to that role, Dr. Salmon was director of the Division of Nursing for the United States Department of Health and Human Services, leading the key federal programs aimed at shaping the nation's nursing workforce. In her previous academic experience, Dr. Salmon was professor and chair of Public Health Nursing in the School of Public Health at the University of North Carolina; she also headed the Public Health Nursing Program at the University of Minnesota, where she began her academic career. Her areas of teaching and research include health policy and administration, public health nursing and health workforce development. Dr. Salmon is the author of numerous publications in these areas. She has also been extensively involved in the area of international health, beginning early in her career with a Fulbright scholarship focused on national health systems development in Germany and Kuwait. Since then, she has worked with a number of international organizations, including the World Health Organization, International Council of Nurses, the Pan American Health Organization and the W. K. Kellogg Foundation. In addition, Dr. Salmon has consulted with governments and organizations outside of the United States and served as a member of the U.S. Delegation to the World Health Assembly. In her national leadership roles, Dr. Salmon is a member of the Board of Trustees of the Robert Wood Johnson Foundation and she has been involved in a number of key advisory groups, including the White House Task Force on Health Care Reform. She was also the chair of the National Advisory Council on Nurse Education and Practice. In these and other roles, Dr. Salmon has led in the development of a number of important national initiatives aimed at interdisciplinary workforce planning, enhancing diversity in nursing and meeting the needs of underserved peoples. Dr. Salmon has received numerous awards and recognitions, including membership in the Institute of Medicine and the American Academy of Nursing. Dr. Salmon received her doctoral degree from The Johns Hopkins University School of Hygiene and Public Health, holds degrees in nursing and political science from the University of Portland and is the recipient of two honorary degrees. Dr. Salmon has also been a Fellow in the W. K. Kellogg National Fellowship Program and the Hubert H. Humphrey Institute of Public Affairs.

We are talking about "Big Nursing."
Coin the phrase. Make it yours. Use it,
and you will be provided the opportu-
nity to explain what the term means
to those who need to know.
                              —Vernice Ferguson

2

NURSING, YOUR TIME HAS COME!

Written by Vernice Ferguson, RN, MA, FAAN, FRCN

How do we continue to grow and know as we do our work? One way, which is commonplace today, is through mentors. Another avenue is by accessing others in a more formal way, the written word. The writings of others and being mindful of their words are powerful tools that enable us to keep growing and knowing.

I gave these remarks at the opening session of the annual conference of the National Nursing Centers Consortium in 2004, a consortium comprised of nurse leaders in nurse-managed health centers. The remarks conclude with comments about leadership accessed through reading, for regardless of the work setting where nurses find themselves, leadership is required.

In my reading, I came across some heartening news in *Health and Health Care 2010: The Forecast, The Challenge,* prepared by the Institute for the Future and funded by the Robert Wood Johnson Foundation. This publication describes the healthcare workforce and its future supply and demand.

> In many ways, the nursing profession is the most qualified to respond to current changes in the health system. Nurses' training focuses more on the behavioral and preventive aspects of healthcare than does that of physicians. Their skills are increasingly in demand in an environment that is moving toward outpatient care and requires its healthcare providers to function as teams and assume managerial responsibilities. (2003, pp. 102-103)

Yes, nursing, your time has come! Nursing as a profession has the core values to lead the healthcare industry. Nurses possess the foundational competencies which are critical to lead the healthcare industry. You who provide services to people in nursing centers prove it every day in the work you do as community nursing clinic leaders. You are so appreciated by those you serve.

Now, it's time to get out the word to all those who do not yet know this; it's time for "Big Nursing."

Big Doctoring and Big Nursing

In my reading, I came across a book titled *Big Doctors in America: Profiles in Primary Care* (2004) which led me to the concept of "big nursing." Fitzhugh Mullan, MD, left government service in 1996. He believed he had come too far from his early career as a primary care pediatrician. He had done policy work in the U.S. Department of Health and Human Services' Public Health Service, had headed the National Health Service Corps, and had served on President Clinton's Healthcare Reform Task Force, along with other duties. Wanting to recapture his roots as a practitioner, Mullan went to work part-time as a primary care pediatrician at an inner city health center in Washington, D.C. In an interview, he was asked to define the term "big doctoring." His response was that he wanted a term to capture the essence of primary care. He reflected on what it takes to be a "big doctor." For him, it is both a skill set and a mindset. Mullan reminds us that primary care clinicians function as partners with patients. He continued, "The role of the primary care clinician is going to be like that of an air traffic controller. They help people make decisions to arrive at the place they want to be." He believes that primary care is the bedrock of a good healthcare delivery system.

Those of us working in healthcare every day know this, but others do not. Translation and reinforcement of this message is sorely needed for policy makers and payors, as well as a larger public. They need to understand that your work is indeed the bedrock of a good healthcare delivery system. You represent the best there is in a troubled, complex, and dynamic system. All of us are counting on you to lead us to a healthier future. Your time has come!

Yes, Your Time Has Come

Yes, your time has come, and there is something to be gained by each of us. Your time has come to frame the issues for those who need to know and appreciate what you do to improve the public's health each day as you assist people in taking charge of their lives with confidence.

We are talking about *"Big Nursing."* Coin the phrase. Make it yours. Use it, and you will be provided with the opportunity to explain what the term means to those who need to know.

Your time has come for you to demonstrate your commitment, your competence, and your selflessness as you effect positive healthcare outcomes in the daily work that you do.

About Leadership

Trying to lead while the system itself is being reshaped puts a premium on brains—brains to imagine the possibilities outside of conventional categories, to envision actions that cross traditional boundaries, to make new connections or invent new combinations. This is the attitude you must embrace and an action imperative that must become yours.

I am a nurse who served in leadership roles for most of my career, so I know a thing or two about it. One thing I know well is that leadership is critical to success. You may well have the finest clinical skills as well as business acumen, but it is all compromised if leadership qualities are not apparent.

I'll borrow from *Leadership*, a book I read by Rudolph Giuliani, and outline the five principles Giuliani believes are common to leaders in any line of work:

1. **A set of beliefs and knowledge of what they are.**

2. **Courage.** Courage is feeling fear and being able to overcome it. Some words I will remember for a long time were offered by a religious sister in Philadelphia who works with vulner-

able people. She said, "Faith does not give you the answers, it gives you courage."

3. **Relentless preparation.** If you prepare for everything else relentlessly, you will be able to respond to the unexpected as if intuitively—as nurses, you do this daily.

4. **Teamwork.** Nurses are recognized for their ability to work in teams.

5. **Communication.** You must be able to talk to people and express what you believe.

The challenge of leadership has always been to provide coherence, structure, and ultimately meaning in times of great change and dislocation, surely characteristic of our present and expected future.

Displaying leadership is critical to your work. Continue to develop the traits characteristic of leaders as you hone your clinical skills and business acumen. Each is essential to assure your success as a leader.

CONCLUDING STATEMENT

Consider these words of advice from a fourteenth century monk, quite suitable for these times.

> Brother if you are in ecstasy, exalted by St. Peter and St. Paul or whatever example you wish to take, and you hear that the sick are in need of warm soup, or any other assistance, I hereby give you counsel: Leave your meditation immediately, come down to earth and warm the soup. (Walker, 1957).

Indeed, each of you is focused, caring, and outcome-oriented. What you do each and every day is to offer "any other assistance," and even warm the soup.

You have come down to earth. You have been there all along. You are the connection, the bedrock, for so many here on earth who need you and have come to appreciate you. Keep up your very good work and keep pushing—pushing those whom you serve to take charge of their lives with confidence and assurance—while you continue to push other healthcare professionals, policy makers, payors and people of good will—to join you as they too come down to earth to warm the soup or offer any other assistance.

Keep up the "big nursing."

REFERENCES

Giuliani, R. (2002). *Leadership*. New York: Hyperion.

The Institute for the Future. (2003). *Health and health care 2010: The forecast, the challenge*. Princeton, NJ: Jossey Bass

Mullen, F. (2004). *Big doctoring in America: Profiles in primary care*. Berkeley, CA: University of California Press.

Walker, V.H. (1957, January). Nursing functions and actions. *American Journal of Nursing*. 57(1). 79-80.

(See page XVIII for biographical profile.)

"Failure is not fatal; it can be character building."
—Honorable Phyllis W. Beck

3

TEN LESSONS I LEARNED FROM MY CAREER

Written by Phyllis W. Beck, JD

1. Recognize Discrimination

Most women don't recognize discrimination even when it stares them straight in the face. I graduated from Brown University with a pretty good academic record. My first job was at Time, Inc. where I was being trained as a researcher. The magazine stories were pulled together by a researcher, a writer, and an editor. The writer and editor were higher in status and paid more money than the researcher. The writers and editors were all men. All the researchers were women. Certainly, as was later shown, women were perfectly capable of doing the same work as men. It did not occur to me until years later that this hierarchy was discriminatory and sexist.

Later, in the 1970s, a group of women at *The New York Times* and *Newsweek*, where similar situations existed, took legal action. For the first time, I realized that not only had I been in an unfair environment, but I had accepted it *because that was how it was always done.*

2. What You Look Like—and What You Wear— Defines You

At *Time,* women who were secretaries or in the business department were well groomed. In the editorial section, where I was, women would dress casually and carry dirty raincoats. In an elevator full of people, it was easy to identify which women were secretaries or in the business department, and which women were editorial and put together stories in the magazine.

3. Prepare to Achieve Your Goal

After my stint at *Time* and a short career as a local newspaper reporter, I happily stayed home for 10 years with my four children.

In addition to motherhood, I volunteered at the children's schools and for the Democratic Party. I soon realized that I would never rise in politics, or in any other way, unless I had specialized training. I would be pasting stamps on envelopes for the rest of my life. So, I decided to undertake graduate work and prepare for a career. I was encouraged by Betty Freidan's book, *The Feminine Mystique*.

4. CUT YOUR LOSSES

I initially enrolled in graduate school at Bryn Mawr College in the psychology/child development department. Try as I may, I could not find a comfortable home in that subject of study. One night, while complaining to a friend of mine that I hated my studies, she got a little tired of my grousing and asked me the crucial question: "What would you have done if you were a man?" The question stunned me, and I had no answer, but I thought about it for several days. I realized that many of the young men I knew from my undergraduate work at Brown University had, like me, majored in political science. Unlike me, they had then gone on to law school. A light bulb came on, and I began thinking about law school. The idea seemed absurd. It was 1962; I was responsible for the care of four children and a husband. I knew of no other woman in law school and really had never known a lawyer, male or female. However, I persevered and enrolled in the night division at Temple Law School. From the first night of law school, I knew it was for me. In retrospect, cutting my losses by withdrawing from Bryn Mawr was the right thing to do.

5. FAILURE IS NOT FATAL

The lesson from law school that stands out clearest in my mind is that *failure is not fatal; it can be character building*. In my student days, professors seemed obligated to call a student to her feet and then show her and the rest of the class that she didn't know anything. When questioned by a professor using the Socratic method, I fell on my face, or made a fool of myself. But, I found it was not fatal. Sure it hurt; but I picked myself up and moved forward. After a while, failure hurts less and less. I find that once I accept the possibility of failure I can try more new things, take chances, and be freer. I don't have to play it safe—and that's liberating.

6. Pay No Attention to Other People's Opinions

Since I was the only woman anyone knew in law school, social acquaintances felt perfectly free to criticize my decision to attend law school. So-called friends, and even my pediatrician, warned that my children would come to no good. Without saying it, these people made it clear I was no good because I broke a taboo by going outside my expected roles of mother and wife. I recall one evening when I was on a panel with an established lawyer. He chastised me, asking how I could expect my children to turn out well when they were deprived of the smell of chicken soup on a Friday night.

The Delaware County Bar also expressed its disapproval. In those days, before an applicant could take the bar exam, she had to be approved by a Bar Association's ethics committee. The first time I appeared before the committee, they did not approve me. How could a woman with household responsibilities and four children be morally fit if she attended law school? A second committee was assembled. They approved me. I passed the bar examination.

7. Select the Right Weapons

The weapon I selected for my first experience in practice was competence. I worked with a black lawyer in a medium-sized firm, and most of our clients were black businessmen. The clients and I were mutually respectful, and I worked with them as a no-nonsense professional.

When the firm began to break up, I went to work as the only woman in a large, prestigious all-white firm in Philadelphia. The environment was totally different. Neither the partners nor the clients knew what to make of a woman lawyer. I tried a variety of weapons: competence, manipulation, and confrontation. I don't think anything worked. It would take another 10 years before the old-guard legal establishment accepted women.

I eventually taught at Temple Law School and then at the University of Pennsylvania Law School, where I was vice dean. Competence was again my chosen and appropriate weapon.

8. Stand Up for What You Believe

When I was at the all-white, all-male establishment law firm, the firm had its meetings at the Union League, which at the time was an all-male preserve. I attended my first firm meeting by trying to enter the Union League through the same entrance as my male colleagues. Two male ushers grasped my elbows and escorted me out. I could only enter by the women's entrance and thought this was grossly discriminatory. It wasn't until the second, and then the third, woman joined the firm that the firm agreed to move the meeting to another venue.

Economic hard times ultimately caused the Union League to consider taking women as members. I had a lively and public debate via "Letters to the Editor" at *The Legal Intelligencer,* stating my position that the Union League should accept women. The contrary position was expressed forcefully in letters, as well. The Union League eventually accepted women and asked me to join, but I declined.

9. Go for the *GOLD*

While working at the University of Pennsylvania Law School, I learned that the superior court, the intermediate appellate court in Pennsylvania, had been expanded from 7 to 15 members. Governor Dick Thornburgh had eight appointments to the court; four Republicans and four Democrats. Established in 1895, no woman had ever served on it. I decided it was about time the situation changed and applied for the job.

I appeared before a nominating commission that the governor had established. I prepared for the interview in the same way I prepared for my law school exams. I tried to predict the questions and I formulated answers in advance. The nominating commission did forward my name to the governor. He nominated me. Now I needed to be confirmed by two-thirds of the state senate. Although I had been a Democratic committee member and had twice run for local office, including at the local school board level, the senate members concluded I didn't have enough political connections. The senate refused to bring my name to the floor.

With the legislative session over, the governor re-nominated me. I lobbied intensely for myself in Pennsylvania's capital, Harrisburg, to no avail. I could not break through. Then I read in the newspaper that one of the leaders in the general assembly from Philadelphia had been deposed from his leadership position. I went to see him. I introduced myself to him as one loser to another. We had a long and meaningful conversation. When I left, he said he would support me, and I could tell everyone about his support. I shall always be grateful to Representative Joe Smith because he broke the logjam. My appointment was confirmed. Afterward, I was elected for a 10-year term and then won a retention election.

10. RECOGNIZE AND GRAB OPPORTUNITY

In 1993, I was asked to join the board of the Independence Foundation. Susan Sherman, who is now president and CEO of the foundation, came on the board at the same time as I did. The Independence Foundation has given us the opportunity—I should say privilege—of "growing" the non-profit community. One of the best and most satisfying projects we have undertaken is our support for nursing. It has given me great satisfaction to watch nursing expand, to realize all of the underserved people it ministers to, and to be associated with nurses—a group whose dedication and commitment is beyond what I have seen in almost any other field.

If opportunity arises, grab it, and run with it even if you think at the time there is not another thing you can fit into your life!

These are the "Ten Lessons I learned From my Career."

PHYLLIS W. BECK, JD, is a magna cum laude graduate of Brown University. She earned a JD from Temple Law School night division in 1967 where she was first in her class. After practicing law, she taught at Temple Law School and then was vice dean at the University of Pennsylvania Law School. Since 1981, she has been a judge of the Superior Court, the intermediate appellate court in Pennsylvania. Initially appointed by Governor Thornburgh in 1981, she was elected statewide to a 10-year term in November 1983 and retained in office in 1993. She was the first woman to serve as a judge on the court which was formed in 1895. Judge Beck is known as a strong advocate for judicial reform. As chair of the Governor's (Casey) Commission on Judicial Reform, Judge Beck authored a 260-page report recommending major structural reform in Pennsylvania's Judicial System. Since the late 1980s she has been actively pursuing judicial reform. The nationally recognized American Judicature Society awarded her the Herbert Harley Award for her leadership role in the field, especially her work with Pennsylvanians for Modern Courts. Her scholarly articles, published in a variety of law reviews, reflect her interest in criminal law and issues relating to women, the family, and equality, among others. She is a contributing author to a book on the Pennsylvania Constitution. She is chair of the Independence Foundation, the ninth largest foundation in the Delaware Valley. She is vice president of the Free Library of Philadelphia. She was a founding member and president of Philadelphia Futures, an organization devoted to mentoring children. She is currently on the board of Philadelphia READS, the local initiative of the national program of America READS, and the board of the After School Activities Partnerships (ASAP). She is a member of the American Law Institute, the Committee on Judicial Ethics of the Philadelphia Bar Association, a board member at Villanova Law School and Temple Law School and the American Judicature Society. She also serves on the board of the Mann Center for the Performing Arts. She is an Overseer of the University of Pennsylvania School of Nursing and a board member of the Museum of American Jewish History. She is president of the Foundation for Cognitive Therapy and Research. She is the recipient of two honorary degrees, the Judicial Award of the Pennsylvania Bar Association, the Anne X. Alpern Award of the Pennsylvania Bar Association's Commission on Women, the Brennan Award of the Philadelphia Bar Association, and the Florence Murray Award of National Association of Women Judges, the Outstanding Alumni Award from Temple Law School, the Pennsylvania Legal Services Excellence Award, and the Sandra Day O'Connor Award. She is married to Dr. Aaron T. Beck. They have four children and eight grandchildren.

When you are a nurse, there is no limit
to what you can be.
—William Warfel, RN, CNAA, PhD

4

NURSING IS GOD'S WORK: AN INTERVIEW WITH WILLIAM WARFEL

Written by Tine Hansen-Turton, BA, MGA, JD

The World Has Changed for the Good

Bill Warfel got his introduction to nursing in the U.S. military in the 1960s. He was in the United States Navy for five years as a medical corpsman. When he became aware of all that nursing offered, he chose to pursue a nursing degree. It was particularly the navy nurses who inspired Bill to think about becoming a nurse, but he had to figure out how to overcome the resistance to men as nurses. In those days, men did not enter nursing. Instead, they went to medical school. Nursing was considered a female profession, and men stayed away from it. The few that did go to nursing school gravitated toward more technical aspects of the job or toward administrative roles with little direct patient interaction. "The world has changed for the good," according to Bill, as more men are going into the nursing profession and doing direct patient care.

Find the Right Mentors

Early on, Bill realized there are two keys to becoming successful: finding the right mentors and having the right boss. Bill credits his success to two mentors, Dr. Clifford Jordan, a professor at the University of Pennsylvania School of Nursing, and Carol Hutelmyer, a Certified Registered Nurse Practitioner. Mentors help cultivate your confidence and belief in yourself. Most people are not aware of their potential for success. Mentors are those rare people who take notice and realize untapped potential. A mentorship is a continuous evolving relationship with someone you admire who supports you in growing into your potential.

When asked how you find a mentor, Bill said it is simply "darn luck" that it happened for him. Some people are easier to mentor, and some mentors think they are mentors but are not. For Bill, mentors reminded him where he was going, pulled him in when he needed it, and knew when he needed them. They are in your corner, always reliable and loyal. For him, the real proof of a mentor relationship is in the results. But, as a mentee, you have to be willing to build your own skills, and be humble enough to see the world in a different light.

Having the right boss is equally important to finding the right mentor. To be successful, your working relationship with your boss is critical and should inspire trust, allow for you to make mistakes, and let you be successful. Bill had the good fortune to work for a woman who offered him all this and more.

The right boss will give you the flexibility to grow. Bill worked at Einstein Hospital for 26 years under Susan Bernini, the director of nursing. She was building a new organization and hired Bill on the spot to grow it with her. Bill had a special bond with Susan. This did not mean they always agreed, but they had an enduring respect and trust for one another. Behind closed doors, they could disagree. Once they left the room, they were united. Bill always looked up to Susan and says without hesitation that she is brilliant, devoted to the organization, and always made him want to do the right thing.

The Only Constant in My Life is Change

When asked how he stayed 26 years in one place, he said that healthcare and the institution were changing at all times. To maintain the energy and excitement, it has to be changing. Bill stayed because the organization was changing, and he wanted to be in the forefront to make sure it went in the right direction

Bill took the lessons learned from his mentors and evolved into precepting nursing students. Throughout his career Bill has mentored graduate nursing students—with an open door policy—and would let them in on the darkest secrets of hospital administration issues with the understanding that they would learn the importance of confidentiality. He became the most sought after preceptor among nursing students and has mentored many nurses.

YOU CANNOT LET "BEEN THERE, DONE THAT" GET IN THE WAY

Life after retirement has proven to be an excellent vehicle for Bill. He recently traveled to Oman to teach students there about healthcare issues. As wise as Bill feels, he says, "You cannot let the 'been there and done that' attitude get in the way. Keep trying new and old things that may not have worked because of timing and change. Maybe the environment has changed."

He has learned that there are regional norms dictating what you can do. For him, his work in Maine, as interim vice president, was different from his role as vice president of patient care services at Einstein. Bill has learned that in management, there is no right way—there is a lot of gray—and the challenge is that everyone thinks *their* way is the right way.

ON HEALTHCARE POLICY AND THE FUTURE OF HEALTHCARE

"The system is broken." Bill says that the right answer has not yet been found. The number of uninsured continues to grow and the healthcare system is fragmented. You need a conductor in the system to orchestrate the care delivery. Managed care, but not necessarily managed care organizations, can have a positive impact when done correctly. So far, America has not found the right balance. The financial structure has changed, and the way we practice care is better, but we have different levels of providers, all of which are fragmented from one another. Nursing has a bright future in shaping health policy and the overall direction of the fragmented healthcare system.

NURSES DO GOD'S WORK

Nursing has the public's confidence. Nursing has a bright future because nurses do good work, and say some, God's work. Bill believes one of the beauties of nursing is its diversity and ability to adapt quickly to new changes, which is often not realized until one actually works in nursing. This is nursing's strongest card. To date, it has adapted the best of all healthcare professions to changes in population health and healthcare demands. Thus, nursing's role will grow and primary care responsibility will be on the shoulders of nursing. Right now nursing education is superb. Healthcare and surgeries are being done in outpatient settings with fewer and fewer hospitalizations, and many procedures are even being done in the home. The way healthcare is going, acute care will become critical care and be provided in less intense, more cost-effective settings.

Nursing has been a joyful career for Bill, a minority figure in nursing. "When you are a nurse, there is no limit to what you can be. Once I became a nurse, I never looked back; I never had a day when I did not want to go to work."

WILLIAM M WARFEL, RN, CNAA, PHD. With 35 years experience as a healthcare professional, numerous publications, and a doctorate degree, William (Bill) Warfel offers in-depth knowledge of the healthcare industry. Bill served in the U.S. Navy as a medical corpsman. He then worked for a number of healthcare organizations as a staff nurse, including the Presbyterian University of Pennsylvania Medical Center and Graduate Hospital in Philadelphia. Bill joined Albert Einstein Healthcare Network as Assistant Director of Nursing in 1976 and was later promoted to chief nurse and executive associate general director. Bill served as vice president of Patient Care Services from 1997 until his retirement in 2002. In addition to his professional experience, Bill was an active member in various professional organizations such as the American Organization of Nurse Executives and the National League for Nursing. From 1994 to 1995, Bill served as president of the Southeastern Pennsylvania Organization of Nurse Executives. He is the recipient of numerous awards from professional organizations. He is a member of the Honor Society for Nursing, Sigma Theta Tau International, and is a Fellow of the Johnson and Johnson Wharton Program in Management for Nurse Executives. In May of 2006 he was honored by the Maimonides Society of the Albert Einstein Medical Center for his years of service. Bill earned a BS in nursing and a PhD in philosophy from Temple University. He also earned a BA from La Salle University and a MS in nursing from the University of Pennsylvania. Since his retirement in 2002, he has been consulting for IMA, Inc., Chadds Ford, Pennsylvania, in a number of healthcare institutions, sometimes filling interim positions. He also spent eight months in the Middle East as adjunct faulty for Villanova University. Bill lives in Little Egg Harbor, New Jersey.

II

LEADERSHIP IS ... CHALLENGING

As I talk about what it was like being the president of ANA, please think about leadership and politics. Think about how this relates to race, age, sex, power, leadership, mentoring, conflict, organizational politics, pressures and influence. Think about Darwin's theory—the fittest survive.

—Barbara Nichols

5

A PERSONAL
LEADERSHIP ODYSSEY

Written by Barbara Nichols, DHL, MS, RN, FAAN

Leadership is a topic that interests most women in general, female nurses in particular. As women, we are intrigued with the power associated with leadership and often driven by the challenge to capture it. I welcome this opportunity to share my experiences and tell how I became president of the American Nurses Association (ANA) in 1978. During the late 1970s and 1980s, American women were excelling in sports, entertainment, and in medicine. For the first time in history, women reached new heights in the corporate world. In 1978, Hannah H. Gray, a German-American, became the first president of a major research university—Chicago University. In that same year, seemingly out of nowhere, Nancy Lopez, a Mexican-American, became the star of women's professional golf. Like these women, I also faced new challenges and choices in the unfamiliar terrain of leadership. As such, my insights are gleaned from the school of hard knocks. My comments speak to leadership positions in general, especially for women of color. It is my hope that the analysis of my leadership role, as president of the ANA, will prove to be both informative and instructive.

At some point, we all have asked: What is it that makes leaders? How do I get into a leadership position? And once there, what is it that sustains one in a leadership role? These reflections could be titled, "The Pressures, The Passions, and The Process." However, the real story is that as the first black president of the ANA I was forced to survive. The firsts are always forced to survive. My goal here is to provide my perspective which, of course, is individual and relative.

As I talk about what it was like being the president of ANA, please think about leadership and politics. Think about how this relates to race, age, sex, power, leadership, mentoring, conflict, organizational politics, pressures and influence. Think about Darwin's theory, *the fittest survive*. Please note that if you are a minority, overcoming stereotypes and collective guilt is the underbelly of success.

This is because there are always those who believe that you are in a particular position of leadership because of affirmative action policies and quotas. While often affirmative action policies help place minorities on the path to leadership, it is competent performance that grants staying power. The challenge for all minority leaders is to figure out how to be a success but not a "sell out." In my case it was how to maintain my individuality, but not abandon my spirit of black community. How to be black, but integrated, whole, and yet always part of the collective nursing community?

What then is power? Power is the ability to influence who, what, when, where, and how things get accomplished. Think about the need for power, the scope of power, the extension of power, in its relationship to leadership. Think about the economics of power, the costs of power (psychological and financial), and the opportunities afforded by power. In this context, the ingredients for power must consist of desire, broad thinking, possession of some form of capital (be it money or even an asset such as education), the ability to sacrifice, and on occasion, neurotic behavior.

I was elected the president of ANA in 1978, and re-elected in 1980. I served two consecutive, two-year terms and completed my second term in July 1982. I was the first black nurse in the 100-year history of the ANA to seek and win the United State's highest nursing office. My supporters were confident that I would succeed, and my opponents anticipated my failure. I felt the burden to over-achieve in order to gain the respect and confidence of the majority.

It is no secret that to be a black, female nurse in a leadership position is to experience bias, prejudice, and stereotyping based on ethnicity, gender, and occupation. Nor is it a secret that to be a nurse who is bright and confident is to experience harassment, jealousy, and resentment based on occupation and class bias. As a black female in a healthcare leadership role, you will never be sure whether the response you evoke is tied to prejudices about blacks, women, minorities, nurses, or even your independence. In large part, survival depends on the development of a healthy paranoia; hence, your tempered neurosis.

However, to wallow in the quagmire of bias, prejudice, and stereotyping is ultimately linked to the ingredients for defeat; as it is to become so arrogant that you think yourself above the quagmire, and to become so relaxed that you forget that conspiracies do exist. When you have experienced this situation, you will understand that utopia is not necessarily found at the top. I conclude from my experience that for women and minorities to excel in leadership positions they must manage these factors with grace. They must come to understand that in reality, some form of bias, prejudice, and stereotyping is always insidiously or blatantly present.

The points I have been making are not based on esoteric theories. They are, rather, based on my own real-life experiences. As nurses, a profession dominated by women, we seem to have forgotten that experience can be a valuable teacher. Equally valuable is separating myth from fact. Allow me to point out some of the common myths that relate to blacks in leadership:

Myth #1: Being black and female gives you an edge.

Myth #2: Black women get jobs over white women.

Myth #3: Race gives black women an advantage.

The reality is that being a double minority gives you more to overcome. While it is true that black women have increased their income, educational levels, and status in white-collar professions, white women outnumber black women two to one in the workforce.

When considering the leadership style which has served me best, I recall another myth, being that democracy facilitates progress. Democracy is a political philosophy in which individuals only decide on *who* will assume control of their destinies. It is not a theory of leadership growth based on the needs or wants of the populace. Participatory democracy, on the other hand, is an excellent theory of leadership in that it does not degenerate into a popularity contest, resulting in a better course of action because sovereignty is established first and foremost.

In a participatory democracy, collective goals become transparent and individuals are forced to participate while they are held accountable for their politics and choices. For example, a hospital administrator who presides according to participatory democracy is carrying out the transparent will of the entire staff, and every employee is held responsible for his or her part in that process. The democratic vote of a distant board cannot begin to address the infrastructural needs of such a hospital or, in this context, any other healthcare facility.

Doctors, nurses, aides and other support staff need to play an active role in decision-making. Not just in deciding who will ultimately make the final decision, but continuing (as a rule) to participate in the decision-making processes which effect day-to-day operations and the long-term goals of the organization. Charisma, which in my opinion is ambiguously defined and overstated as a leadership characteristic, becomes less important in this instance where leaders are seen as facilitators rather than dictators. In fact, more than 50 years of study on leadership has failed to produce one personality trait or set of qualities that can be used to differentiate between leaders and non-leaders.

When I announced that I was going to run for the presidency of ANA, only two states supported me: Oregon and Wisconsin. The Wisconsin nurses seemed to support my ideals and their devotion to a common cause was fascinating. Further, when we consider participatory democracy, these nurses were actively involved in my campaign on all levels, from raising money to lobbying for me across the country. They provided immeasurable psychological, physical, and financial support from beginning to end.

An interesting difference emerged, however, when I asked the Oregon nurses why they supported me and they expressed that they didn't really know. They simply followed the lead of their executive director. For their sake, we can only hope that I met their expectations as an effective and worthy leader. At the time of the election, I was a member of the ANA board of directors. However, not one board member supported me. The board members stated that I was not old enough, I was not experienced enough, that I was not ready, and that I did not look "presidential."

The bylaws of the association at the time stated that to be eligible to run for office one must be a member of the association and willing to serve if elected. It contained no reference to age or physical appearance. Thinking back, I have always wondered why women in leadership positions are held to different standards. We are all guilty in the sense that upon first thought we imagine female leaders to be older, faceless, and rigid. The truth is that all women, regardless of color, are virtually frozen out of influential positions in the corporate, governmental, and academic world if they are slightly quirky, young, attractive or ethnic, and fun-loving.

A point of advice: to be successful in any endeavor, you must learn the art of capitalizing on your individuality, but more importantly learn to be a thinker. Stay several steps ahead of your adversaries and get behind your allies. Learn how to use intuitive elements of survival in order to achieve success. This, I believe, will serve you longer than any other physical or personality trait.

If you have not had the advantages of the elite, you can still rise to the head of the class. It may take longer because you may not have role models or access to shortcuts. Yet, in my case, no groundswell of folks stepped forward to help me learn the ropes. I learned from my own experience.

I ran against two nurses with doctoral degrees, Dr. Marian Murphy, then dean of the University of Maryland School of Nursing and Dr. Laura Simms, a professor at Cornell University and then-president of the New York State Nurses Association. I was billed as the candidate of no consequence based on the dark horse theory—the candidate that is hardly known. Ironically, among blacks I was also touted as not being the "dark horse" of choice. I was not the black of choice because I did not wear an Afro, nor had I marched in Selma. I reminded blacks, like it or not, I was the only black choice they had. In meetings with many state delegations, the questions asked most frequently were: "If elected, would I only represent blacks?" And, "If elected, would I only appoint blacks?" Of course, my response was, "Certainly not! I would represent all of nursing." Yet, to blacks I was not black enough and to whites, perhaps I was too black.

Does this orientation toward a minority or female candidate reflect the persistent stereotypical notion that the life experiences of minorities, in particular, and women in general, do not prepare them for leadership? Or does it mean that being a minority automatically suggests a life of infinite struggle and undeserved consequences? In answer to this question, my seeking reelection in 1980 surfaced an interesting dynamic. Although, I was nominated by 12 states and six organizational units of the association, my appearance (unopposed on the ballot) was challenged by a past ANA president. This past president sent a letter to the 50 states suggesting that surely there were other qualified nurses more suited for the nursing profession's highest office. Thus, my opponent was nominated from the floor, at the ANA Convention.

For the first time in the history of the ANA, an unopposed, incumbent president was challenged from the floor. In the tradition of the organization, this is considered to be a tasteless act. It was an act, however, that worked to my advantage. Considering that a nomination from the floor is another form of participatory democracy, this challenge had a silver lining and sweetened the victory when I was reelected in 1980.

The presidency of the largest nursing organization in America is a grand and personal odyssey. It offers excitement, status, prestige, and immeasurable opportunity to experience the depth and breadth of nursing, but also the formulation of health policy in this nation. I am forever indebted to the nurses of America, who granted me the privilege to represent them.

What have I learned? On a personal level, I have learned that others do not necessarily desire that you become successful; often because the personal success of one can suggest the subservience of others. For this reason, I am convinced that success is not handed to anyone on a silver platter. One must learn how to accept rejection while holding on to personal goals. Learn to be self-motivated. Learn that it is imperative to have knowledge and skills and essential expertise as it relates to issues and trends in your professional field. Learn to appreciate all aspects of the programs you will manage and supervise. Know that the road to success is paved with isolation, social and domestic sacrifices, feelings of vulnerability, exhaustion, dual roles, and many sleepless nights.

Finally, be aware that to everything there is a season, with unforeseen storms and sunshine in between. Know that regardless of where you find yourself, eventually you will have to leave the mountain top. When that time comes, leave not with bitterness or despair, but leave with the joy of having had the opportunity to experience the view from the top. I've learned an invaluable concept about power. I've learned that power is not a commodity like money, or something that one can accumulate and store up for use whenever one likes. You must use power while you have it or you will lose it.

Experience has taught me that when it is all said and done, companies, organizations and governments do not really grant titles and powers to women because they are kind and good, or even as a mandate for affirmative action. Women get powerful leadership positions because they are ambitious, competent, intuitive, patient, and persistent! Power is the control, impact, and influence you demonstrate on a moment's notice—unrehearsed, original, and against all odds. I have always been powerful. Being elected president of ANA was just another manifestation of that reality.

Thank you for the opportunity to share my perspective on my leadership experience. I have tried to challenge your assumptions about leadership at all levels of nursing and relate my experience and ideas to nurses who desire to tread new paths as leaders.

Barbara Nichols, **DHL, MS, RN, FAAN,** is currently the chief executive officer of the Commission on Graduates of Foreign Nursing Schools, an immigration-neutral, non-profit organization founded in 1977 and based in Philadelphia, Pennsylvania. The Commission is internationally recognized as an authority on education, registration, and licensure of nurses worldwide. Through its program of services, it implements international educational standards and regulations. Prior to holding this position, Nichols served as professor of nursing at the School of Nursing, University of Wisconsin, Madison, and as director of nursing for the Wisconsin Area Health Education Center System. She has held a cabinet position in Wisconsin State Government and is a former International Council of Nurses board member and a president of the American Nurses Association. Those positions enabled her to develop a broad perspective on nursing education, regulation, and practice. As Secretary of the State of Wisconsin, Department of Regulation and Licensing, she was responsible for seventeen (17) boards that licensed and regulated 59 occupations and professions. This job entailed accountability for the development and implementation of policy, programs, and services that responded to regulatory issues, initiatives and reform. She is the author of over 70 publications on nursing and healthcare delivery and has received numerous awards for contributions to the nursing profession. She is the recipient of four honorary doctoral degrees for her scholarly work. She holds a diploma in nursing from Massachusetts Memorial Hospital, Boston, Massachusetts, a baccalaureate degree from Case-Western Reserve University, Cleveland, Ohio, and a master's degree in behavior disabilities from the University of Wisconsin, Madison, Wisconsin. She is married and the mother of one daughter and identical twin sons.

The underserved are not just the poor or uninsured but include all those who get only pills and procedures instead of time and attention, all who are treated in parts and exist in the mind of the clinician without a face or name, all who are talked at but not listened to, all who are denied nursing care (not nursing services, nursing care), and all who are discharged as "cured" but not healed.

—Veneta Masson

6

TAKE HOME MESSAGES

Written by Veneta Masson, RN, MA

You couldn't cast a more unlikely pair for the roles of doctor and nurse in a small, inner-city clinic. In 1976, when we began, Jim was a research pathologist headed for a career in academia. I had recently been transferred to Washington, D.C., from Brazil, to become director of nursing for Project HOPE, an international health organization. Jim spent his days in the lab studying lobsters. I spent mine traveling to program sites in Latin America and Africa or poring over plans, budgets, and staffing projections at headquarters. We met in church one Sunday after Jim, inspired by his volunteer service rehabbing apartment houses for low-income tenants, sounded a call to establish a health ministry in one of Washington D.C.'s poorest neighborhoods. This will be my hobby, I naively thought, a way to keep in touch with hands-on nursing in the United States as I continue to work in the field of international health.

Jim, with the meticulous preparation and dogged determination that characterizes the best researchers, led the task force that formed in response to his call. Over the course of several months, we honed in on our objective, which was to start a clinic that would provide primary healthcare to people of all ages and care for the elderly and disabled in their own homes. It would be organized as a non-profit corporation. Unlike the few free and volunteer-staffed clinics in Washington D.C. at that time, we would support ourselves with third party payments and fees for service on a sliding scale supplemented by donations and small foundation grants. We'd stretch our budget by keeping professional salaries low while paying support staff at market rates.

With the inevitable drift and disaffection among task force members ("Why can't we offer legal services, too?" asked the lawyer. "What about community organizing?" asked the activist. "Why must we charge for our services?—God will provide" said the idealist), Jim and I were the only health professionals left on the task force. By then we had located a townhouse in a run-down neighborhood at the frayed edge of the federal city. Its residents were certifiably poor, uninsured, and underserved: A perfect spot for our clinic. We named it Community Medical Care (CMC) and opened our doors in September 1978.

Jim's role was clear from the start. He would serve as half-time physician and director. In the early days of the task force, he had cobbled together an unofficial family practice residency to shore up his primary care skills. Now he was ready to diagnose and treat the illnesses of the patients whose names would appear in each 15-minute slot in the appointment book.

I had planned to continue at Project HOPE, working at CMC whenever I could. But within two years, I'd resigned from Project HOPE to take advantage of the unique opportunity and professional challenge I felt our new venture afforded me. Neither Jim nor I had any preconceived notion of what a registered nurse would do in our setting. Because my master's degree was in community health nursing and preventive medicine, I assumed that I would handle health teaching, community outreach, home care (where I had solid experience), and some administrative tasks.

It didn't take long before our patients were telling us what they wanted. For example, a Muslim woman with a gynecological complaint would only permit another woman to examine her. Alas, we had no female physician. A Central American immigrant who had trouble explaining what was wrong with him asked to see someone who spoke Spanish. That would be me, but I wasn't equipped to examine or treat him. For our home-care patients, most of whom suffered from a number of chronic illnesses, nursing care was definitely primary, but they also needed their medications adjusted, lab tests monitored, and acute problems evaluated. Jim could do these things, but here I was, already in their home. With the exception of children who were brought in for their shots, few of our patients seemed interested in preventive healthcare—or teaching or counseling. They wanted a quick fix for their present crisis before they lurched on to the next one. And they longed to have their own private doctor, something virtually unattainable in clinics open to the poor and uninsured.

I saw that I was going to need continuing education. As a nursing student in the 1960s, I'd never had a course in physical assessment. Fortunately, I found what I needed at Georgetown University, not far from my home. The skills I acquired in physical examination allowed me to expand my practice. But while I was doing a well-baby exam, the mother would inevitably ask me about his cough, rash, or recent bout of diarrhea. And it seemed like every time I did a routine pelvic exam, my patient would mention a vaginal discharge, pelvic pain, or odd change in her menstrual cycle. An older man whom I'd been helping with his diabetic diet ("health teaching and counseling") would ask me how to adjust his insulin dose in order to avoid the weak and dizzy spells he'd been experiencing. I sighed, signed up for more classes and entered into an informal apprenticeship with Jim. I was steadily incorporating more of the science of medicine into my practice of nursing.

By now, I'd heard about nurse practitioners. Although I didn't know any personally, I'd read about them in the nursing literature. Their arrival on the scene had caused quite a stir throughout the nursing leadership ranks. For some, nurse practitioners were the perfect answer to the need for more and better primary healthcare. For others, the emphasis on medical diagnosis and treatment represented a betrayal of nursing principles. Nurses, they claimed, did not diagnose and treat; they assessed and intervened. Nurses did not address medical problems, but human responses to these problems. Curing was not the nurse's concern; providing care was.

Eventually I met Betsy, a colleague of Jim's from his days volunteering at the local free clinic. If Betsy hadn't been a nurse practitioner (NP), I decided that she'd be running an ICU somewhere. Smart, quick, and confident, she'd engage Jim in shop talk about the fine points of diagnosis, treatment, and prescription. I was impressed but felt I wasn't the same kind of nurse as Betsy. I was a community nurse, the low-tech, high-touch kind. And I had my pride. Even though I had taken over from Jim as clinic director after the first three years and was managing the complete care of many of our patients, I felt our peer relationship would be jeopardized by the collaborative agreement with a physician required of nurse practitioners in the early 1980s.

Despite my attempts to correct them, many of my patients referred to me as Dr. Masson ("my private doctor") because, in their view, what I did was doctoring. Our medical assistant was the nurse: she took their history, checked their vital signs, performed lab tests, listened to their problems, explained things, and gave good advice.

It was only when I finished combing through Washington D.C.'s new Nurse Practice Act in the mid-1980s that I realized I could no longer continue to do what I was doing under my RN license alone. My professional liability insurer was asking questions about scope of practice. I'd also begun to overhear Sharon, our patient care coordinator, refer to me as the nurse practitioner. When I called her on it, she rolled her eyes and said, "Look, you have to learn to be flexible. What you're doing is what an NP does and people are beginning to understand the NP role. How else am I going to describe you?"

It was time to push the envelope. I applied to the post-master's family nurse practitioner program at the University of Virginia.

After completing it, I felt able to offer my patients even more than I had before. The staff complained: I was taking longer in the exam room, sometimes more than the 30 minutes we had settled on (because it was agreed that nursing takes more time than doctoring and includes the careful listening, teaching, counseling, and preventive care at which nurses excel). Sharon became expert at sorting out which patients would benefit most from the time and attention I could give them, and which had problems that could be more efficiently handled by Jim with his highly focused expertise in solving specific medical problems.

In time, we hit our stride. For many years, we remained a small, stable staff: doctor, nurse practitioners (Teresa, who came to us as an NP student from Catholic University, stayed on after graduation), patient care coordinator, and medical assistant. On our best days, we felt like family. On the others, we simply did the work we were committed to. We eked out a living and reaped a bountiful harvest in human relationships and as witnesses to healing.

During the 17 years I was part of CM, I learned a number of lessons that I hope will prove useful to others who share my interest in decent, affordable, and personalized healthcare for those we call underserved. I call them my take-home messages.

1. The mom-and-pop stores that dot most inner-city neighborhoods provide a good model for primary healthcare. A conversation with one of our patients, who owned a corner store near the clinic, prompted this comparison. CMC, like Columbia Grocery, was small, personal, located in a residential area and offered credit and a familiar array of what my patients called "the main things." In place of Pampers, Tide, microwave sandwiches, sodas, and beer, we offered shots, pills, check-ups, cures for garden variety illnesses, and help with the more complex ones. Most striking of all, we had mom and pop in the roles of nurse and doctor.

2. **To compare the complementary roles of nurse and physician to mom and pop may seem stereotypical, but it is useful in describing the blend of nurturance and problem-solving required for effective and holistic healthcare.** Good nurses know something about doctoring—and good doctors know a thing or two about nursing. Both understand that there will always be a large, shifting, gray area between nursing, which I define as healing through care and nurture, and medicine, the diagnosis and treatment of disease. Any time professional tensions arose between Jim and me, we could address them creatively because we were unhampered by the rules, customs, and job descriptions characteristic of large organizations.

3. **Small is beautiful and personality is essential when serving people who have trouble navigating the massive, complex, and dysfunctional organizations of which the U.S. healthcare "system" consists.** Too many people get "lost in the aisles" of our windowless medical warehouse stores. They don't know how to ask for what they want, use the goods they are sold, or return what doesn't work. They can't afford to shop in advance of need. They are ill-served by institutions that crank out health services as if they were products and regard patients as customers.

4. **More is not better except when it comes to spending time with patients and learning to understand the big picture.** Too often, a person who has had no healthcare at all is catapulted into a complicated course of treatment that is financially, culturally, and personally unsustainable. I think of my patient, Ruby, early in the course of her diabetes. During a hyperglycemic episode, she'd gone to the nearest emergency room, where she had been admitted to the hospital. She was discharged on tight diabetic control with a "weigh and measure diet" and a complex schedule for insulin injections and blood glucose testing. She couldn't (or wouldn't) prepare the prescribed foods,

handle the multiple daily injections of two different types of insulin, or purchase the supplies needed to check her glucose levels four times a day. Her expensive hospitalization in the care of highly skilled professionals had not served her well. At CMC, we were able to stabilize her condition reasonably well on one injection a day, a "rule of thumb" diet, and frequent contacts to bolster her resolve. We became expert at giving first class second class healthcare.

5. Good healthcare, by itself, will never result in healthy communities. The environment, adequate food and shelter, meaningful human relationships, and healthy life styles are vastly more important in determining the well-being of a population. I also like what Washington Post columnist Courtland Milloy wrote during the crisis provoked by the closing of Washing D.C.'s public hospital, that "...scars on the souls of black folk cannot be treated in hospital emergency rooms, but removed only with spiritual scalpels wielded by a community of people who care." In my experience, that applies not just to "black folk," but to all who suffer.

6. Except in a crisis, healthcare is never the most important thing. For those sitting on what we called the "wino bench" down the street, the most important thing is the next taste of booze. For many of our families, it's to get through one more day—pay the rent, put food on the table, make sure the children go to school—survive. For our kids, at any given moment, it's not learning to "say no" to drugs or sex or dropping out of school—it's social security (not the kind you get from the government), friends, and fun. For my patient, Sheila, her high blood pressure and diabetes were never a priority, but flagging down a taxi to take her to CMC ("not the emergency room, no, not there!") as she began slipping into shock after a bee sting, was.

7. You can't separate preventive and curative services. People respond best to health counseling when they are sick or scared. A young man, Derrick, comes in with a stomachache. I find out that his girl-friend has just gotten pregnant. He's lost his job and his health insurance along with it. His mother has kicked him out of the house. Is this the time to talk about safe sex? Maybe not, but one thing is for sure, it's the only possible time because I won't be seeing him again once he feels better and leaves the office—until he comes in with his girlfriend to show off their baby, that is.

8. **To be effective, health workers in rough-and-tumble neighborhoods must expect to experience and work amidst the same chaos that reigns in the lives of their patients.** There's Darlene in her motorized wheelchair outside the clinic, parked at the bottom of the steps. She sends her grandson Joey in to tell us she's out of all her medications—has been for "a while." Between patients, I go out on the sidewalk for an impromptu consultation, blood pressure cuff, stethoscope, and prescription pad in hand. Then I schedule a home visit. At CMC, on any given day, we were faced with countless missed appointments, walk-ins, and "failures to comply." We coped with exam rooms full of out-of-control kids ("Sorry, I don't have a babysitter.") and adults ("Snooky, you really can't lie there on the waiting room floor all morning.") This is life. You learn to deal with it.

9. **Sometimes it's not that people are underserved, but that services are under-received.** I think of the Clinton administration's push to make more vaccines available to clinics like ours. It didn't address the real problem, which for us was getting children to the clinic to receive the vaccines. Our refrigerator was well stocked. But even their favorite nurse, Teresa, standing outside the front door of one of her large, extended families, offering door-to-door service to the clinic to get the children up to date on their shots, couldn't always get an answer to her knock.

10. The underserved are not just the poor or uninsured but include all those who get only pills and procedures instead of time and attention, all who are treated in parts and exist in the mind of the clinician without a face or name, all who are talked at but not listened to, all who are denied nursing care (not nursing services, nursing *care*), and all who are discharged as "cured" but not *healed*.

Is CMC a model I can recommend? Probably not. For us, the bottom line was a call to serve, not to earn. We wanted to satisfy our patients, not a group of shareholders. We focused our efforts on a few thousand souls in a neglected section of the city. Even so, we did not turn a sick neighborhood into a healthy one. True, some found healing at CMC. And we were able to provide a handful of patients with meaningful jobs. One of the most important lessons I learned was that all of us, professionals and so-called support staff, working together with respect and tolerance for our individual and professional strengths and limitations, had potential for healing far greater than any of us working alone.

VENETA MASSON, **RN, MA,** practiced as a registered nurse for 35 years in communities, homes, and hospitals in the United States and abroad. In 1978, she helped to found a small, inner-city clinic in Washington, D.C., called Community Medical Care. For the next 17 years, she was both family nurse practitioner and director of CMC. She also began to write essays and poems from her clinic experiences. Since leaving Community Medical Care in 1995, she has published two books: *Rehab at the Florida Avenue Grill* is a collection of poems about some of those patients whose lives changed hers and *Ninth Street Notebook—Voice of a Nurse in the City*, winner of an *American Journal of Nursing* Book of the Year award for 2001, contains lessons, stories and reflections on nursing and healthcare. Since leaving practice in 1998, Masson has continued to reflect on and write about nursing and healthcare. *She is currently the proprietor of Sage Femme Press and serves as a contributing editor of the American Journal of Nursing.*

"A powerful leaning tool, which I used
continuously, was the learning and growth
that comes from reading and reflecting."
—Vernice Ferguson

7

ROLE MODELING FOR LEADERSHIP THROUGH LESSONS LEARNED AT HOME

Written by Vernice Ferguson, RN, MA, FAAN, FRCN

I am an African American woman born in North Carolina of southern African American parents. My father and his father were ministers. My mother, who was a school teacher, was the only child of a school teacher. Her father, a butcher, died three months before her birth. As an only child of a young widow, her uncles were most generous as she grew up, assuring adequate money and clothing through her college years. She told us of the trunks of clothes that she took away to school and the antics of those years in the early 1920s, the flapper era. Early on, and throughout my childhood, my parents spoke of their college years. There was never a question of us, my two brothers and sister, going to college.

In the stormy 1960s, my older brother, a Harvard Law School graduate of the 1950s, served as the dean of the Howard University Law School. With great pride, my mother told us that one of her uncles was in the first graduating class of Howard's law school in the 1890s.

COMING OF AGE

I grew up in Baltimore, Maryland, during the era of racial segregation. Public accommodations for blacks and whites were separate and unequal. Schools, stores, and neighborhoods were all black. Dominant in the lives of the oppressed were three institutions: the family, the church, and the public school. In each of them, support, encouragement, and the strength of endurance sustained us all.

I grew up following the Great Depression, an economic downturn and a time of hopelessness for many Americans. Shortly thereafter, World War II and full mobilization of citizens left at home and soldiers alike took center stage. All of us, children and adults, were engaged in the war effort. My father served as an air raid warden while my mother served as a Red Cross volunteer, visiting the troops and dispensing donuts, coffee, and the like. As school children, we purchased U.S. government bonds. Rationing was the order of the day. It affected all of us.

In spite of the many demeaning acts that permeated my childhood and early adult years in a segregated society, there were positive occurrences. First, with few opportunities for people of color, the pubic schools often had first-rate teachers who had no opportunities for employment in the larger society. I was most fortunate to have had outstanding public school teachers, many of whom were products of middle class homes and had the privilege of attending outstanding colleges and universities in the north. It was not uncommon to have teachers with advanced degrees, including doctorates, in the public schools. We looked to teachers, preachers, and physicians as significant role models and mentors.

In our home, two rooms were very special: the guest room and my father's study. Because blacks could not stay in the major hotels of the south, guests of my parents stayed in the guest room and dined with our family. Meal times were quite special for the food, conversation, and guest interactions. We were afforded so many expressive opportunities to listen and to be heard as children. The study, filled with reference books, encyclopedias, the Harvard Classics, an unabridged dictionary, and books written by and about politicians, was a treasure. My father spent hours reading in the study each day. The Ferguson children completed book reports and home work there. There was even a duplicator. I recall my older brother using this machine to make campaign flyers when he was running for class president in high school. During my years in high school, I was always on the honor list. Not to be outdone, my older brother would opine, "Boys are late bloomers."

THE COLLEGE YEARS

Because of segregated schools and our desire to attend excellent schools, each of us left Maryland to attend college. All of us were grateful for the opportunities afforded us and the sacrifices of our parents.

Ever since the fourth grade, I had wanted to become a nurse. My mother was a frustrated nurse "wannabe" who was denied that opportunity. Her very proper Victorian mother held the belief that nurses ran after doctors while secretaries ran after their bosses. Her only child became a teacher who fulfilled that role in the early years of marriage and later became the solid rock for us at home.

Of all of the visitors to the Ferguson home only one was a nurse, a public health nurse in Washington, D.C. When she came to visit, she regaled us with stories about her work. Another budding nurse, a nursing student at the local black hospital, served as our baby-sitter when our parents were traveling. I remember Miss Roberts with fondness. She did not cook well, but she made great refrigerator frozen desserts, and she was young.

It was clear that I would pursue my desire to become a nurse in a collegiate setting. I graduated with honors from the five-year program at New York University Bellevue Medical Center in 1950.

AT WORK AS A NURSE

I found my first job in the classified ads of the *American Journal of Nursing* and considered it particularly attractive because it promised no rotation of shifts. Having just married and become emancipated from rotating tours as a nursing student, Montefiore Hospital in the Bronx, New York, was the ideal place to begin my career. I was chosen as the first registered nurse to head the six-bed metabolic neoplastic research unit. While there, my first publications appeared in the *American Journal of Nursing* and major scientific journals. I was privileged to present one study at an annual meeting of the Federation of the American Society for Experimental Biology. My engagement with the physician scientists and other team members, chemists, dietitians, and physicists continued, along with publica-tions, for many years after I left the group.

Being a clinician and staying close to the bedside in hospitals was always important to me. Even after becoming a chief nurse in a Veterans Administration (VA) setting, clinical practice and its improvement were high on my agenda. It was my reason for being and a way of making a major impact on how patients were cared for and nurses stretched to provide excellent care.

STRATEGIES FOR SUCCESS FROM LESSONS LEARNED

I was a nurse administrator in the federal (VA) healthcare system with strong ties to academic institutions—a federal chief on the Washington scene, at the Clinical Center, National Institutes of Health, and the assistant chief medical director for Nursing Programs at the Department of Veterans Affairs, responsible for the largest organized nursing service in the world. I had a good measure of success with unparalleled opportunities and challenges in these assignments.

During my administrative years, I was primarily responsible for hospital-based nursing care in inpatient units. In these settings, the seat of power existed in well-organized medical services. Hierarchical organizations prevailed with minimal interdisciplinary focus; silos dominated the scene, each with its own way of doing things. Shared governance in nursing had not appeared. Partnerships across disciplines were rare, most often non-existent. Quality assurance programs were just emerging with the nursing profession providing leadership.

I welcomed the emerging opportunities for a powerful and excellently performing nursing service with new choices for staff nurses to be heard and interdisciplinary interactions. Developing a consultation service for nursing at the Clinical Center, and giving voice to young nurses, brought such satisfaction and continued praise. At the Veterans Affairs Central Office, a staff nurse came to the office for a year, with special input from her on personnel practices and construction of workspace, thereby setting a new standard and by example, a new expectation at all facilities.

While in the VA leadership position, I went on sabbatical leave for six months, again to inform nurses that they, too, could access this opportunity just as physicians did in the system. It also sent the signal that each of us must continue to grow and know. On my sabbatical, I focused on geriatric care and gerontology, an acknowledgement that we were entering an era where aging mattered. As the leader, I needed to become knowledgeable if I wished to be credible.

One important learning sequence option, so important for executive leaders, is access to other leaders. For some, mentors and role models exist. For many others, formal and informal peers are helpful to the leader of an organization. For many of my generation, and as a minority nurse, significant role models and mentors were nonexistent. Hence, trial and error and growing from mistakes as my course was corrected were often the case. A powerful learning tool, which I used continuously, was the learning and growth that comes from reading and reflecting. Reading beyond the nursing literature predominated in my life, including the reading of biographies and autobiographies of both famous and infamous people throughout history. Yes, even reading the obituary page in a major newspaper has always been a part of my reading for on the death of notable people, facts are learned and, on occasion, cautions or corrections in one's own life plan are indicated.

Reading beyond the nursing literature included books and journals from business and even military strategists for some of their axioms of warfare are transferable to nursing. Consider, for example, *Strategy*, by the late Sir Liddell Hart. In his book, he listed eight axioms of strategy in the art of warfare. Three are listed here:

1. **Adjust your end to your means.** In determining your object, clear sight and cool calculation should prevail. It is folly to bite off more than you can chew.

2. **Keep your object always in mind while adapting your plan to circumstances.** Realize that there are more ways than one of gaining an objective.

3. **Choose the line (or course) of least expectation.** Try to put yourself in the enemy's shoes and think what course it is least probable he will foresee or forestall.

Hart further addresses all those means used in grand strategy: fighting power, financial pressure, diplomatic pressure, commercial pressure, and ethical pressure. Applying ethical pressure was evident when stockholders protested Nestlé's practice of sending powdered milk to developing countries where mothers fed their infants using contaminated water—for that was all that was available. Or black families in the 1960s who boycotted department stores as Easter approached. They refused to buy spring clothes from segregated stores thus applying financial pressure to effect change.

Sun Tzu in *The Art of War* addressed warfare and five circumstances in which victory may be predicted:

1. He who knows when he can fight and when he cannot will be victorious.

2. He who understands how to use both large and small forces will be victorious.

3. He whose ranks are united in purpose will be victorious.

4. He who is prudent and lies in wait for an enemy who is not will be victorious.

5. He whose generals are able and not interfered with by the sovereign will be victorious.

Tzu's 2400-year-old book is reportedly required reading in some companies. Mao Tse-Tung was strongly influenced by Sun Tzu and began to apply his strategies successfully against General Chiang Kai-Shek's naturalists as early as 1930.

The 1960s were a stormy period of protest and tumult in the United States. One observer of those times wrote an article in the *Saturday Review of Literature*. What captured my attention as I read it was the title, "How Could Anything So Bad Be So Good?" Farson suggested strategies gleaned from the 1960s for solving problems not previously known. He suggested five useful strategies;

1. Instead of trying to reduce the discontent felt, try to raise the level of quality of the discontent. (By shifting the focus on not ignoring the concerns, redirect it to higher order focus).

2. Instead of trying to "cool it" in a crisis, use the time of crisis to make major changes and improvements.

3. Instead of trying to make gradual changes in small increments make big changes.

4. Instead of trying to improve people, improve environments.

5. Instead of looking for professional elite for the solution to any social problem, look to the greatest resource available within the very population that has the problem.

I have always aimed in my work to be a change agent, so needed in the healthcare delivery system, especially in nursing where innovation, vibrancy, and excitement needed to occur. Reading and reflecting on the literature of change, and how to effect change responsibly, was always important to me. Knowledge was gained, tools developed, and analysis of what worked, what needed to be refined, and what needed to be discarded, were always at the fore. Even though in retirement, I continue to access others' thoughts through reading, for it is my principal avenue of continued learning and growth.

Power and influence are intriguing concepts. In Washington, D.C., the city in which I live, their appearance and study are readily apparent. Robert Greene, in his book, *The 48 Laws of Power,* addressed the writings of men and women who have studied and mastered the game of power. These laws span a period of more than 3000 years and were created in civilizations as disparate as ancient China and Renaissance Italy, yet they share common themes. These laws have a simple premise: certain actions almost always increase one's power, while others decrease it and even cause ruin. Greene's book is instructive. I have shared his ideas when I am on the speaking circuit so that others can learn from these laws.

One anecdote I like to share is power. One day there was a horrendous rainstorm. Trees were falling and power lines were down all across town. A junior senator's wife called a senior senator's wife during the course of the storm and asked, "Do you have power?" The senior senator's wife responded, "Over whom my dear?"

REFERENCES

Farson, R. (1969, September 2). How could anything so bad be so good? *Saturday Review of Literature*; 20-2.

Greene, R. (1998). *The 48 laws of power*. New York; Viking.

Hart, B.H.L. (1975). *Strategy*. 2nd revised edition. New York; Praeger.

Tzu, Sun. (1989) *The art of war*, Edited with a foreword by James Clavell. New York; Delacorte.

(See page XVIII for biographical profile.)

It is from my faith that my vision of leadership, as well as my endurance for the journey, have been established and continually reenergized.
—Beverly Malone

8

My Leadership Journey

Written by Beverly Malone, RN, PhD, FAAN

I grew up in Elizabethtown, Kentucky, a small country town where the farm animals outnumbered the people. I was raised by my great-grandmother, Ms. Addie, who was a healer for the community. When I wasn't in school, I was in church and the Baptist Church has had a significant influence on my life. It was there I learned about tribulations, storms and other crises and received fair warning that life is full of these natural and unnatural disasters. It is from my faith that my vision of leadership, as well as my endurance for the journey, have been established and continually reenergized. When I was younger, I was certain I did not want to be a leader. While spiritually the foundation for leadership was being laid, in the context of my young reality it seemed like an unnecessary burden. I just wanted to survive and grow up.

But there was always an angel on my shoulder, even when I was avoiding the call of leadership. That angel took many forms at different times. It was Mrs. Sadie Tate, my excellent fourth grade math teacher in a segregated school system, who told me that I was smart like my mother and grandmother who'd both been her students before me; or Ms. Douglas, my sixth grade teacher whom I met right after the schools in "E'town" were integrated. Ms. Douglas was my first white mentor and followed my progress through high school, meeting with me periodically in the town square to review my academic progress and reward only my "A" grades with $.50 each.

My mentors have come in all shapes, sizes, and colors. There was Agnes, a black hospital clerk, who was empowered to do all the scheduling for the psychiatric nursing roster. I noticed that I was receiving an unusual amount of night duty every week and questioned Agnes about the rationale for this. She patiently explained to me that she chose to do it. In turn, I responded that I would educate my way out of having an overabundance of night duty. Agnes always claimed credit for my doctoral preparation. On reflection, I can definitely say she was one of my mentors.

It was not until I was working on my master's degree in psychiatric-mental health nursing, though, that I realized I wanted to be a leader. I not only wanted to be, but *had* to be a leader. This revelation came with and through a mentor, Dr. Hildegard Peplau, the mother of psychiatric-mental health nursing. Learning from and with her, my horizons and vision moved to a higher plane of desire. Her validation resurrected the foundation for leadership that had been formed by all my early mentors. Working with Dr. Peplau was traveling with a leader, and I realized the road I was on was a road to leadership.

After working as a clinical nurse specialist and faculty member in psychiatric nursing, I decided to return to school for my doctorate. By this time, I had a husband, a two-year old little girl, and a brand new baby boy. This was a difficult period for our family. Before I graduated with my degree in clinical psychology, I had become, through a divorce, a single parent with two very young children.

While pursuing my doctorate, however, I met one of my lifelong mentors, Dr. Hattie Bessent. She infiltrated my life, encouraging and daring me to higher achievements along my journey. Dr. Bessent is a psychiatric-mental health nurse who successfully led the American Nurses Association's Ethnic and Minority Fellowship Program, producing more than 200 doctoral-prepared minority nurses. I was one of those fortunate enough and blessed enough to know her.

She introduced me to political power by offering me the opportunity to work as an intern in Washington, D.C. I was so excited! I was going to work with Patricia Harris, the Housing and Urban Development secretary. Several weeks before I was due in Washington, however, Dr. Bessent sent me a letter saying that my assignment had been changed to Senator Inouye, the senator from Hawaii. I was devastated. I felt I must have been considered not good enough for Secretary Harris. I asked Dr. Bessent about the reason for the change and she responded that I had been selected by the senator. I privately assumed that she just didn't want to tell the hard truth. This was an early time in our relationship, and I didn't know that Dr. Bessent never withholds the plain truth. In fact, she is one of the most direct leaders I have ever met. This experience with the senator would whet my appetite for politics and governmental involvement and leadership.

When I finished my doctorate, my daughter was six-years old and my son, four. The next step was to determine my direction of travel. I reviewed my vitae and realized that while I had been consulting to management during my graduate education, I had no management experience. I decided to become a director of nursing, working for a colleague who had an MBA/MSN. Some of my friends cautioned me about stepping back by working for someone who did not have a doctorate and below my degree. This advice made no sense to me. I was the one without management experience. This was my opportunity to learn from others who were more prepared in my deficit area. Education does not determine someone's worth.

I was soon promoted to assistant administrator for nursing and for six years worked with budgets and management at the frontline. The experience was invaluable and would play a significant role in my leadership journey. It was during this work that I realized that my clinical background and education had prepared me to lead with creativity, knowledge, and passion.

Leveraging this experience of real management and leadership, I was overly confident about my calling and my ability. My next challenge brought me back to the reality and the difficulty of leading. A colleague recommended me for the position of dean of nursing at North Carolina Agriculture and Technical State University (NCA&T), a historically black university. It was a small program with a diminishing faculty and student body. I smugly felt that I could easily run a small school of nursing after managing a large cadre of nurses in a major university hospital. However, I did not know that leading a faculty is one of most difficult and tedious initiatives.

Once again, friends and colleagues suggested that my leadership journey should not be delayed by including a historically black university. Yet this part of my journey would prove to be incredibly successful for me professionally. NCA&T's School of Nursing faculty and student body was tripled in size and reputation; I was inducted as a fellow of the American Academy of Nursing; and, during my tenure, I had the opportunity to serve as interim vice chancellor for Academic Affairs. I really wanted the position. Unfortunately for me, NCA& T produced more black engineers than any other program at that time so it was a fellow dean in the School of Engineering who won the position. By not being selected for the vice chancellor role, I turned my attention to the position of president of the American Nurses Association (ANA).

This stage of my journey allowed me to work with several giants who were all committed to my election. Let me introduce my campaign managers: Jeanne Marshall, a political strategist akin to those who run presidential campaigns for the nation; Dr. Janice Brewington, my associate dean at NCA& T and a "let's get it done" organizer extraordinaire; and Dr. Hattie Bessent, my lifelong mentor who was steadily working behind the scenes. With this team I was destined to be successful, and they engineered my election twice with grace, humor, and skill.

At this point, I was not sure what my next step should be. The ANA suggested that a government position would be a constructive bridge for nurses and the association. Within weeks I was offered the position of deputy assistant secretary for the U.S. Department of Health and Human Services with a portfolio that ranged from international health to genetic testing and food and drug safety. It was a challenging move that included working with then Surgeon General David Satcher, who was responsible for the first mental health report for the U.S. I left my ANA presidency six months early to assume this new and exciting position. It was a productive year that emphasized my skills as a psychiatric clinical nurse specialist with the resulting outcome being the first national plan for children's mental health.

This was the last year of President Clinton's administration, and I campaigned vigorously for Mr. Gore. After the election, I cautiously started to look around for other opportunities. While I was looking, the fantasy post came into view. I heard through the international grapevine (Dr. Hattie Bessent, local sponsor) that Christine Hancock, then general secretary of the Royal College of Nursing (RCN) was leaving and there was a wide invitation for applicants. I put my application forward, without much effort or attention, since it was only a fantasy; surprisingly, my application kept moving until I was a finalist. Being offered the position and accepting it was one of the most dramatic decisions of my life. How could the RCN want an American, an African American, to run the most prestigious professional nursing trade union in the world?

I knew it must be a mission with spiritual authority and direction. My job was not to question why, but to accept the position and get on with the work. My biggest challenge was a total lack of networks. In the United States, I had multiple networks meeting a variety of needs. In the United Kingdom (UK), I had no strong relationships or professional networks to facilitate moving political, professional, or personal agendas. Fortunately, Bill Clinton gave me a sign of support and approval in talking with Prime Minister Tony Blair and Gordon Brown, chancellor of the Treasury. I never knew the details, but whatever momentary exchange occurred was worth its weight in gold. The overall political agenda for the RCN was manageable and within the first two years we were able to accomplish the most comprehensive pay and career upgrade for nursing that had occurred in recent history.

To some, I was a foreign object in the U.K. body that needed to be expelled. There was an extensive campaign to damage my reputation and to send me back to the states. I found myself in the media on a frequent basis. While some of the media was positive, there was a steady stream of complaints ranging from my mother's operations and accusations of queue jumping to my attendance at a Labour party reception which was interpreted as a partisan stance on my part. None of the individual complaints had any validity to them; but the continuous flow steadily eroded my council's confidence in this American. So, after little more than a year in the post, there were some calling for my resignation. By keeping my eyes on my mission and remaining in a professional posture at all times and with the grace of God, I weathered the storm and emerged intact and thriving. There are some things I could have done better or at least differently. The key things I would do differently are:

1. Build my base of support with the nurses and managers away from the organizational center at an earlier point in time. While I accomplished this; it would have been helpful to have done it earlier in my tenure.

2. Listen and decide from my own gut. I was focused on the dissimilarities between the U.K. and the U.S. and assumed that my intuition was U.S.-based. I now believe that my intuition is spiritual and universally based.

3. Negotiate a clearer contract with the organization that included my continuing professional development and travel expenses.

Two years later, I was involved in two learning sets for continuing professional development; one local to the U.K. and the other international. The local learning set has key leaders within and beyond the National Health Service; while the international one, the Praxis Network, has representatives from 11 countries. The local network is particularly useful in filling the gap in my political and professional networks in the U.K. We met four times a year, focusing on mutual problem-solving related to situational crises/opportunities, both professional and personal. The second learning set provided an opportunity for one weekend each May and October to reflect collectively on some issues about work in our professional and societal lives in a thoroughly international setting and in a comfortable space with other professionals.

A very special continuing professional development tool has been my 25-year involvement with experiential organizational learning. I have worked as a consultant in the U.S., the Caribbean, France, and the U.K. This model of learning has a psychodynamic basis exploring how organizations affect individuals and the effect individuals have on organizations. I was recruited into this work by the chair of my clinical psychology program, Dr. Ed Klein, and encouraged to stay by Dr. Rhetaugh Dumas. These two individuals are also lifelong mentors who have touched and transformed my leadership approach and abilities.

Now, let me share with you my lessons learned:

1. **I can be delayed but not defeated.** This is a spiritual mantra that turns every potential failure into merely a delay. It promotes endurance and perseverance and prayer.

2. **It's a cinch by the inch; it's hard by the yard.** I've learned the art of patience, a lesson that frequently requires repeating. It also promotes celebration at frequent intervals of work.

3. **You knew it was a snake when you picked it up.** Be able to identify your enemies. Usually you know them early in the relationship, but frequently we choose to ignore our "knowing."

4. **Don't bleed in the water.** This is advice for when swimming with sharks. Showing one's vulnerability in the presence of enemies can be used in destructive ways against you.

5. **Feed your enemies with a long-handled spoon.** This is the humanistic approach to managing those who may bite the hand that feeds them. They still require feeding, just not too close.

6. **One door closes and another door opens.** This is truly about faith and acknowledging whose hands you are in. When that position that seemed to have your name on it goes to someone else; just be assured that God opens doors that no man can close.

7. **Don't let anyone take your joy from you. The world didn't give it to you, and the world can't take it away.** There are some who believe that they have the power to transform your life from joy to sadness. This is not a valid hypothesis. In weathering the storms of your professional career, your joy valve will need to be located in your soul, where others will not have access to it.

And with these seven learning principles, I must now close. I have miles to go before I rest.

BEVERLY MALONE, PhD, RN, FAAN, is chief executive officer for the National League for Nursing. Prior to this, she served as general secretary of the Royal College of Nursing from July 2001 through 2006. In her clinical career, Malone has worked as a surgical staff nurse, clinical nurse specialist, director of nursing, and assistant administrator of nursing. She was dean and professor of the School of Nursing at North Carolina Agricultural and Technical State University (NCATSU), Greensboro, prior to that. While at NCATSU, she served on the Governor's Task Force on the Nursing Shortage, and was a commissioner of the North Carolina Commission on Health Services. Malone served as president of the American Nurses Association (ANA) (1996-2000) and as deputy assistant secretary at the United States Department of Health and Human Services. She also represented U.S. nurses in the Congress of Nurse Representatives of the International Council of Nurses. During her ANA presidency, Malone served on President Clinton's Advisory Commission on Consumer Protection and Quality in the Health Care Industry and in March 1998 she was appointed to the Health Care Quality Measurement and Reporting Committee. President Clinton also appointed Malone as a member of the U.S. delegation to the World Health Assembly, and she was a participant in the president's round table discussion on the Patients' Bill of Rights. Malone served on the board of directors of the National Patient Safety Partnership, a collaboration with the Department of Veterans Affairs (VA), the American Medical Association, and other national health care organizations. She was the second African-American to serve as president of the ANA. She has been included in Ebony Magazine's list of the 100 most influential African-Americans.

Malone received her BS in nursing from the University of Cincinnati in Ohio; her MS in adult psychiatric nursing from Rutgers, the State University in New Brunswick, New Jersey; and her PhD in clinical psychology from the University of Cincinnati. She has received many honors, including Chi Eta Phi's Mabel Keaton Staupers Award; an Honorary Doctor of Science degree from Indiana University in Indianapolis, an Honorary Degree of Doctor of Science (DSc) from the University of Ulster; the Anthony J. Janetti Award for extraordinary contributions to healthcare; the Distinguished Alumnus Award for outstanding contribution to nursing and society; the Excellence in Nursing Education Award from North Carolina League for Nursing; and the Golden Key National Honor Society's Honorary Member Award, among others.

III

Leadership is ... Collaborative

"When I began thinking about what I would say, I was launched into a life review process. It became clear to me that my trajectory in nursing was one of self-discovery and fulfillment."

—Jill B. Derstine

9

TWELVE JOURNEYS: REFLECTIONS ON A NURSING ENDEAVOR IN SOUTHEAST ASIA

Written by Jill B. Derstine, RN, EdD, FAAN

I was honored and humbled by the opportunity to participate in the "Conversations With" series, and I've looked forward to attending each event and hearing the rich information presented by each person who shared his or her story. Never did I envision that one day I would be sharing my story. When I began thinking about what I would say, I was launched into a life review process. It became clear to me that my trajectory in nursing was one of self-discovery and fulfillment.

Unlike many of my esteemed colleagues, nursing was not my first choice of vocation. I was not one of those girls who "always wanted to be a nurse." I wanted to be a foreign correspondent, a veterinarian, a horticulturist, to name but a few of my many career desires. After two years of majoring in languages at a small college, I changed my mind and headed for a real career—nursing. Attending Johns Hopkins University School of Nursing in East Baltimore was like entering a different world. Born and raised in Bucks County, Pennsylvania, where there was little diversity, I suddenly found myself immersed in a totally different culture where I taught unmarried mothers to breastfeed their newborn babies, carried keys to the locked psychiatric ward where patients screamed inside locked rooms, and washed the backs of the very black men who were lined up in a 10-bed ward.

Community health turned out to be my favorite experience. As I patrolled the streets of inner Baltimore, my heart went out to every family I visited. My community experience occurred around Christmas. I was so moved by the poverty I saw that when I returned home for Christmas break, I convinced my mother to send a big box of my brother's discarded toys and clothes to one of the families.

I graduated, went on to work at a small community hospital and decided right away that I wanted to teach nursing. I went back to school for a master's degree in rehabilitation nursing from the University of Pennsylvania School of Nursing. I loved the long-term aspect of rehab and the fact that people were capable of some degree of independence no matter what their disability.

From that point on, it was many years of teaching that included rehabilitation nursing, medical-surgical nursing, and community health nursing. Along the way, I enrolled at Temple University for a doctorate in Health Education. During this program, as we designed health-oriented programs for persons in under-represented areas, I realized that I had come full circle and was continuing my trajectory which began while working in the heart of East Baltimore in the late 1950s.

Early in 1994, my very dear friend and colleague, Dr. Marie O'Toole, asked me if I would like to participate in a rehabilitation project in Vietnam. At that time, Vietnam was not high on my list of places to which I wanted to travel, but I agreed to go; if it panned out, it would be an adventure, if nothing else. Little did I know that this would be the start of a journey that has spanned more than 10 years and continues as I write these words.

Rehabilitation was nonexistent in Vietnam in the early 1990s. When the United States Agency for International Development (USAID) funded a grant to Health Volunteers Overseas (HVO), I was included as part of a team whose main purpose was to teach rehabilitation concepts to appropriate health professionals in the country. In all, six rehabilitation teams traveled to Vietnam over a period of two to three years, each team dealing with a different clinical entity encompassing spinal cord, amputation, arthritis, pediatric rehabilitation, and neurological deficits. My team's focus was head injury and stroke. Each team was composed of at least a physiatrist, a nurse, and a physical therapist. Our team had an additional member, an orthopedic surgeon. Each team presented one workshop in North Vietnam and one in South Vietnam. Attendees included physicians, nurses, and physical therapists.

Evaluation of the team workshops showed that the Vietnamese nurses had very limited background in rehabilitation nursing knowledge; therefore, those of us who were the nurse member of the teams met and decided to request funds to present a nursing workshop to nurses from all over the country. These funds were granted. From this project, it was found that the basic Vietnamese nursing curriculum was lacking in some areas. An extension of the grant provided the opportunity to link nursing schools in Vietnam with selected schools in the United States, with the objective being to strengthening curriculum development in nursing.

I was now hooked on this project! Having participated in the rehabilitation arm of the project, I began to direct my energies to the nursing education arm. At that time, I was at Neumann College, and I was the first to develop a linkage between two schools—Neumann College and Secondary School No. 2 in Da Nang. For three years I traveled to Da Nang, bringing gifts and letters from Neumann students, and giving lectures and clinical consultation on rehabilitation nursing. The faculty members were my colleagues and my friends, and despite the fact they spoke little or no English and I spoke little or no Vietnamese, we were able to communicate. This was often facilitated with the help of Ms. Quy, the nurse midwife on faculty who had studied in the United States. Sadly, this collaboration ended when I moved to Temple University in 1999.

This move coincided with the development of a new university nursing program at Hue Medical College in Hue City, Vietnam. After a year-and-a-half of negotiations, I developed a linkage between the College of Health Professions at Temple University and the program at Hue. Faculty members from Temple have accompanied me to Hue where we have participated in teaching obstetrical nursing and rehabilitation nursing. In addition, faculty members from physical therapy and occupational therapy have accompanied me to participate in rehabilitation team workshops at Hue Central Hospital.

My mission in Vietnam continues today with a two-pronged effort: rehabilitation and nursing education. In the rehabilitation area, I continue to work with the Rehabilitation Department at Hue Central Hospital. In addition, I correspond via e-mail with one rehabilitation nurse, mentoring her, as she becomes a spokesperson for nursing in the rehabilitation arena. In the nursing education area, with Temple faculty, I continue to work with the faculty in Hue in the areas of curriculum development and evaluation.

I am involved with Nursing Overseas, a program of Health Volunteers Overseas. Through this program, nurses volunteer to serve as faculty mentors in developing countries including Vietnam, Cambodia, India, and Uganda. Within this parameter, I traveled to Cambodia and set up the volunteer program for nurses there.

What does the future hold? The rehabilitation grant from USAID is coming to a close. Outcomes have been so positive that funding has been renewed for each cycle since 1992. The university linkages will hopefully continue after the funding cycle closes. The many indicators of success will serve to keep the project viable. The 12 journeys grew to 14 and will continue as long as there are positive outcomes.

JILL DERSTINE, RN, EDD, FAAN, professor and chair of Nursing at Temple University, Philadelphia, Pennsylvania, has been active in rehabilitation nursing for more than 30 years. A nurse educator with a specialty in rehabilitation nursing, Derstine has been working in Vietnam since 1994 with the focus of introducing rehabilitation nursing to the nurses of that country. She has led several interdisciplinary teams to the country. Several years ago, Derstine negotiated a collaborative agreement between the College of Health Professions at Temple and programs in the Medical College of Hue University. This has resulted in student/faculty interaction in all areas of the nursing program in Hue. She is the author of numerous articles and presentations and is the lead author of *Comprehensive Rehabilitation Nursing*. She serves as chair of the board of directors of the Commission on Collegiate Nursing Education, the national accrediting agency dedicated to baccalaureate and higher degree programs in the United States. In addition she is chair of the Report Review Committee of the board. She received her BSN from the Johns Hopkins School of Nursing, her MSN from the University of Pennsylvania, and her doctorate in education from Temple University. She has served as chair of Nursing in the College of Health Professions at Temple for seven years.

The bottom line is that people and interactions
helped define my empowered leadership. Friends,
colleagues, family, and mentees all over the world
continue to inspire, challenge and support me. To
all of them, I am totally indebted.

—Afaf Meleis

10

LIFE LESSONS

Written by Afaf Meleis, RN, PhD, FAAN

I have selected several empowering themes as the basis for my conversation. I selected these particular themes because many of my life lessons reflect, and are influenced by, these themes. Although there are other themes that describe my life's journey, the fact that I have chosen these particular themes indicates that they continue to frame my life.

If I were to select one theme that describes many of my life's lessons, it would be the power of relationships. Through relationships I learned about different perspectives, diversity in interpretations, the meaning of multiculturalism, and about empowerment to achieve goals and realize dreams. I have been empowered in my leadership roles through the connections and the relationships in my life: family, mentors, mentees, colleagues, research participants around the globe, teams of researchers, and the audiences listening to my ideas, speeches, and teaching. It is through all these connections that I have been able to develop and refine my leadership and how I interact with the world around me.

There are many ways to reflect and present one's journey in life, and there are different ways to capture the different stages and milestones of a journey. We can speak of journeys in terms of people we meet along the way who profoundly influence our lives, and/or we can identify events that tended to keep us on course, events that inspired us to change routes and goals, or events that facilitated our ability to cope with unforeseen and unplanned circumstances along the way. Or we may choose to simply recount our biography without interjecting interpretations, letting the reader develop their own.

The journey I want to share is a mixture of themes that shaped how I see the world, of how I came to order professional priorities and values in my nursing career. Institutions, whether informal or formal, provide structures where relationships are formed, and relationships tend to provide us with lessons that influence how we choose to live our lives. Therefore, my narrative is organized in relationship to those major institutions in which I received formal or informal education. In reflecting on each of these institutional experiences, the themes of diversity, discipline definition, and internationalization emerged to define lessons I learned during my journey. With each of these themes, specific individuals helped to shape and provide the lessons I learned along the way.

Different Perspectives, Diverse Interpretations

My journey began with one profound experience that occurred when I was five years old. I did not learn the lesson from this experience until I reflected on it years later.

I was five years old, living in Alexandria, Egypt, when I heard my grandmother discuss with my mother the *"Tahara"* of our young maid, Farida, who was around 12 or 13 years old at the time. My mother, a 30 year-old nurse and midwife, said a definite "No" to my grandmother, an unusual occurrence of defiance. There was no tension in the conversation. It was just that my mother refused to do what my grandmother suggested. I remember my grandmother saying, *"Ana Hatsraf,"* which means "I will take care of it." She also said, *"Ana Arafa Maslahetha, wana masoulah anaha,"* or "I know what is good for her, and I am responsible for her." I did not know exactly what my mother was objecting to or what my grandmother planned to handle.

The next morning was a holiday time for me, and my mother was not at home. Farida was busy in the kitchen washing dishes. A gypsy went by in the street, and my grandmother called her into our villa. I asked my beloved grandmother why she called the gypsy, and she said so she can read our fortune. She invited the gypsy to our veranda, which was protected from neighbors and surrounded by the fragrance of jasmine and plumeria. I still remember the gypsy's beautiful face, long colorful clothes, dangling long gold earrings, the tattoos on her face and on the back of her hands, matching my grandmother's beautiful green tattoo. I felt safe with this woman.

My grandmother asked her to read my fortune and then took her leave. The gypsy opened her *offa* (basket) and took out lots of beautiful shells which she placed in a very certain pattern on a piece of colorful cloth. She asked me to whisper to the shells and tell them my secrets. She then listened to the shells, threw them around several times and started reading their messages. She was insightful about my young life and about my parents—I was truly fascinated. It was not long before my grandmother came back with our maid, Farida. I still remember Farida smiling and saying "hello" to this gypsy. But, in hindsight, I realized her smile was fake, her body somewhat stiff. She was suspicious, but I did not know why. She seemed anxious to leave the balcony under the pretense of too much work in the kitchen to which she needed to attend. Both my grandmother and the gypsy grabbed her and asked me to leave immediately and go to my room. As I was retreating to my room, somewhat bewildered about the changes of events in this seemingly peaceful morning, I heard Farida's first soft cries. As I closed the door of my room, I heard her scream for what seemed like an eternity, but it was only a minute or two. Then there was silence, except for her moaning and groaning. I ran back to the veranda to see my grandmother hugging and comforting Farida and the gypsy saying, "*Mabrouk*; congratulations, it is done, and it was not that bad." Later, I was to hear my grandmother telling my mother, "Farida jerked her body and I could not hold her still long enough, so the gypsy's razor cut more than it should have!"

I also remember asking Farida what happened, to which she answered, "Your grandmother did to me what my grandmother would have done if she was here. Then she said, "*Ana ethaert*" or, "Your turn will come." She complained of the pain, but she was courageous and she wanted to tell me there is nothing to fear. Despite her obvious pain, she reassured me that it was okay and she would feel better within one week. My grandmother and I took care of Farida. My grandmother took her chicken and chicken soup, a sure sign that she was treated as an invalid. I played with her until she was back on her feet. The last thing I remember about this incident was that my grandmother told my mother that the gypsy bargained for two *Taharas*, but that she told the gypsy my mother objected and that she agreed with her that I did not really need it.

My mother, for whatever reasons, was the pillar in the family who thought of *Tahara*, female genital cutting, as unnecessary. But my aunt from the other side of the family, who was equally educated and a school principal, was uncomfortable with my mother's objections. She agreed to hold off on *Tahara* for her daughter until she turned 18. She consulted with her daughters and her decision finally prevailed. She brought a physician to the house to perform the excision. My cousin bled profusely, but they were afraid to take her to the hospital for fear that the license of this physician would be revoked.

My cousin, a French-educated woman, was like my little sister in spite of the one or two year's difference in our ages. She was far more sophisticated than I, but she never did ask my advice before she was forced to agree with her mother's decision. She never told me how she really felt about her mother or about her decision to accept the *Tahara*. She is now married with seven terrific children.

The "cruel" act of genital excision, which is interpreted as barbaric, described as mutilation, and considered disastrous for sexual relations, is all of that. However, that is not how it is perceived by the kind, loving grandmothers who believe they are doing what they should to protect their granddaughters. Had my grandmother known that the consequences may be bleeding, infection, and infertility, she would have been persuaded not to enforce it. This painful experience taught me my first lesson about diversity of perspectives and interpretations and respect for diversity.

INTERNATIONALIZATION AND MULTICULTURALISM

My professional journey was profoundly influenced by my entry into the University of Alexandria Higher Institute of Nursing in 1957, only two years after it was established by the World Health Organization (WHO) in collaboration with the Egyptian government. With a mother who graduated from a British diploma system and then received the very first Bachelor of Science degree by an Egyptian nurse after completing an RN to BSN degree from Syracuse University of New York, my entire family was supportive of this new form of education. My nursing professors from American, Canadian, and Portuguese universities, as well as non-nursing professors from the University of Alexandria, provided my small class with our first cross-cultural, interdisciplinary, and international experience. We learned how to be comfortable with bilingualism and multiculturalism. All of my earlier experiences in private and public schools with multi-religious peers and multicultural neighborhoods were reinforced by my nursing education.

Although we learned to respect different holiday celebrations, share different habits of eating and interacting, we also learned, in some ways, to look down upon and devalue native lifestyles and healing practices. Seeds of globalization and diversity were planted in my life, but they did not quite bloom yet. Reflecting on that time brings about memories of one of my favorite professors, Florence Hargeti, whom I saw in the United States 20 years later. All through my education, we students knew her only as a "winking" (she always winked with one eye for emphasis) American who was a female and a professor. It wasn't until I saw her in the U.S. context that I realized she was African American.

In my senior year at the University of Alexandria, I was engaged in clinical field work to qualify for a midwifery license. We had finished all the theory portion, including delivery observation and assistance, and it was our turn as senior students to handle the first delivery alone. My Canadian professor was there to lend moral support and ensure I didn't kill a mother and/or baby or did not faint in the process (from fear). I introduced myself to a frightened Sudanese or Nubian woman who was in the expected condition—severely painful labor. I proceeded to the side of the bed to view her genitalia and the arriving baby. I looked at her and emitted an involuntary, unprofessional, and unreassuring scream. What I saw was unlike anything I had seen before or heard about from my Sudanese classmates.

Nothing prepared me, nor my Canadian professor, for what we saw: a wall of ugly scar tissue, two tiny open holes, and distention of the baby's head trying to break out against the wall of scarred tissue. I will spare you the details of her pains and mine, the cutting, the uncertainty, the stitches, and eventually the tears of joy from seeing her—and my—first baby boy born. Nevertheless, memories of the veranda incident came flooding, and instead of judging the Sudanese as "barbarians" who mutilate women with the most severe type of cutting, I was determined to uncover different perspectives, meanings, and different ways to change the practice without devaluing cultural values and practices. The urgency of providing culturally competent care was beginning to take shape in my thinking.

I received a Rockefeller Foundation scholarship to study at the University of California, Los Angeles (UCLA), and so my University of Alexandria phase ended after a year on faculty as a clinical instructor. I left Egypt convinced that I must complete the highest educational degree possible, that I was trained to become a leader, and that life-long learning is a way of life. I entered the United States full of anticipation, eager to learn more about how different minority cultural groups experience life, health, and illness.

UCLA welcomed me with open arms, along with other Rockefeller Scholars from 8-10 other countries. Dean Lulu Wolf Hassenplug, Dorothy Johnson, and Agnes O'Leary opened their homes and lives to us, mentoring us in nursing as well as in American ways of life as we learned about generosity of spirit and openness to internationalism. I was amazed to be met at the airport by Mildred Disbrow (who, subsequently, became a professor at the University of Washington), a total stranger taking the time to meet a young graduate student.

Barely 20 years-old, with limited life experiences, only a BS degree and a year of teaching under my belt, I was totally awed by generous classmates who took me home and made me feel part of their lives. Carole Restovich and Ann Ivey will remain etched in my life forever. It is these experiences that frame my urging of our students, national and international, to open their hearts and homes to each other. The learning environment we had at UCLA has influenced our teaching and clinical work around the world. Ivette Oliveria, a Brazilian president of a nursing organization, is only one example of the impact on us.

Learning About Disciplines and Scholarship

UCLA prepared me for a life of scholarship. I was amazed to learn in the early 1960s that our profession is actually part of a discipline, that research must be driven by a theoretical framework (Burton Meyer), that nurses can be and are theorists who have developed frameworks to define the subject matter of nursing and differentiated it from medicine, and when nurses are prepared at different educational levels they may have different goals. Questioning the fundamental assumptions of the care provided by nurses and connecting these assumptions to the "whys" and the "so whats" of the care was a reminder that critical thinking is vital for achieving evidenced-based outcomes.

Ralph Turner provided me with a solid theoretical basis that shaped how I view people, their roles and interactions, and the kind of research questions and interpretations resulting from the findings. The research I pursued was to answer such questions as the effect of chronicity on how spouses coped with illness and what makes couples able to succeed in planning their families. Roles, interactions, meanings, and responses were the units of analysis as I observed and interviewed participants and their significant others.

The opportunity to teach my first theory course to 35 master's students was provided because Dorothy Johnson took a sabbatical and entrusted me with a unique course she developed. This was practically the first metatheory nursing course in the United States. I owe my metatheoretical interests to this first group of students who challenged and inspired me. A lesson learned: identity in a discipline requires a clear sense of understanding of perspective and boundaries.

My husband, Mahmoud Meleis, completed his PhD at UCLA. Job offers (mine was at the University of California, San Francisco, [UCSF]) uprooted us and our two children (one and three years old at the time) to San Francisco. This is where I began my administrative leadership career, only three years post-doctorate. Within four years, we accepted a temporary move to the University of Kuwait, where I became dean of a community college program with a professional role at the University of Kuwait. In 1975, Kuwait was practically unknown to the United States public and had a population of about 500,000, half of whom were expatriates from around the world.

DIVERSITY AND THE POWER OF SHARED MISSION

The Kuwaiti experience debunked any residue of cultural uniformity myths. Whatever was left of my assumptions and stereotypes about people and their culture was totally blown away by living, working, and experiencing Kuwait. I thought I knew the Middle East well just because I was born and raised in Egypt. I learned the true meaning of diversity as we lived and witnessed the lives of people who came from most of the neighboring Middle East countries, people who were united by Islam, Arabic language, and the values of those who claim Middle Eastern heritage. Though these are group similarities, we soon found out that what differentiated people was their country of origin (Egypt, Lebanon, Syria, Iraq, Yemen, and on and on); their experiences in their own countries and in other countries where they may have lived; their education; their occupations; their family structures; and a whole host of other differentiating factors.

Not only did they perceive these differences, but they also responded differently to situations and events. An example is how Kuwaitis and Egyptians respond and grieve over the death of a loved one, ranging from acceptance, resignation, and moving on to dramatic responses and unending mourning. The former is guided by Arabic and Islamic mandates for the inevitability of death and unacceptability of mourning as it defies God's will. The latter—dramatic responses and unending mourning—is guided by the pharaonic heritage for Egyptians who condone a preoccupation with prevention of death and prolonged rituals and mourning associated with the death of loved ones.

The Kuwaiti multiculturalism, a strong sense of identity with heritage, lineage, and nationalism, was made even more prominent by the laws and services that openly favored Kuwaiti over the non-Kuwaitis and expatriates. Minorities in their own countries and highly unknown to the world in the 1970s, their strong sense of pride in their own identity and nation made them a power with which to be reckoned by all the foreigners and expatriates who controlled healthcare, education, and all the Kuwaiti infrastructure. With admiration I watched the young and inexperienced assume leadership positions over the seasoned veterans only because they held Kuwaiti citizenship, which gave them power that did not defer to years of education and experience. They learned from other countries' experiences not to abandon power to the expatriates and become oppressed and/or ruled in their own country. For me, this was a contrast to my earlier experience as an Egyptian ruled by British colonialism in which Egyptians were continually stripped of their own pride, identity, and heritage. Whereas Kuwaitis insisted on maintaining their Arabic language as the official language and their Bedouin lifestyle as the base of any changes, Egyptians adopted and exalted French, Turkish, and English languages and lifestyles as the preferred standards and strived for all that was foreign made and imported.

I learned many lessons from my two years in Kuwait leading a school of all Kuwaiti students, all expatriate faculty, and mostly rich Kuwaiti infrastructure leadership. Taking advantage of diversity by using it well to enrich all of us required clear communication, careful translation of symbolism and meanings inherent in responses and actions, flexibility to accommodate very diverse work styles and needs, and negotiation to enhance compromises and keep the organization focused on shared mission and strategic goals. Each individual in that organization was part of a family, a community, and a country. As a leader, I was not leading individuals—I was leading families and their countries. All our actions were governed by and reflected collective and embedded cultural values and priorities.

Ultimately, I worked for the Kuwaitis whose love for their own country freed me and allowed me to do whatever I wanted for their institution, their students, and their patients. As long as I kept the welfare of these constituencies front and center, all resources were mobilized, all doors were opened, and no obstacles or barriers were constructed. Other important lessons I learned from this experience: focusing on the goals, being clear about who you are, and making sure there is a universal ownership of the mission and strategic goals.

Back in the United States in 1978, I resumed my professorial role at UCSF. I embraced that role with vigor, opening a new chapter in my leadership without a formal position to define me as a leader. I made a conscious and deliberate decision not to further pursue an administrative career, though I was momentarily tempted when the University of Washington expressed intense interest and invited me for an interview about 1980. After lots of soul-searching, I decided that research, teaching, and clinical practice were where I wanted to spend my energy and time. That is precisely what I did until 2002, when I accepted the deanship at the University of Pennsylvania School of Nursing.

Global Women and Their Health

Differences in how students, patients, and faculties are treated based on their gender, culture, color, socioeconomic status, heritage, and discipline of interest became my major passion. With my research team, I studied how women with low or no income from Colombia, Brazil, Mexico, Kuwait, Egypt, and the United States experienced their work, family, and community, and how their experiences affected their health status. With my colleague, Dr. Juliene Lipson, we developed a primary healthcare initiative called SIHA (Study of Middle Eastern Immigrant's Health and Adjustment). SIHA in Arabic and Farsi means "health." Therefore, the project instantly became well known in the Middle Eastern community. With these women, we studied their health, provided them with health services, listened to their sense of marginalization, and gave them a voice in the healthcare system. With my women faculty colleagues, we developed initiatives to improve the status of women at UCSF.

MENTORSHIP AND LEADERSHIP

Mentorship is vital in advancing careers, but more so for populations who are at risk because of gender, culture, and race. Without mentors in my life, I could not exercise the formal and informal leadership in scholarship and in initiatives that effect change. With this sense of history, I provided vigorous continuity in the cycle of mentorship. Mentees in my life—master, doctoral, and post-doctoral students in nursing and sociology, young colleagues in many fields and others in different spheres of my life—helped me develop my mentorship skills. By declaring me as their mentor, they inspired me to be a mentor. Every mentoring situation left me enriched and humbled as I witnessed my mentees become scholars, presidents of organizations, deans, and leaders of healthcare systems in Egypt, Israel, Germany, Japan, Finland, Botswana, Thailand, Brazil, Australia, Korea, Taiwan, Canada, and the United States.

During our work together, these mentees were members of a network that endured after they left. We studied together, wrote

99

together, discovered together, became enraged together over inequities, and we all did that individually, too. In the end, we remained connected and continued to be part of a large learning environment, and we became critical and understanding of the different models in nursing education.

The University of Pennsylvania School of Nursing is the most recent institution to reflect another stage in my life. Coming east from California (where I had spent 40 years) and from UCSF (a public university), as contrasted with Pennsylvania (an older state) and UPenn (the oldest university in the United States, an Ivy League, private university that practices a responsibility-centered management philosophy) has been inspiring, invigorating, and challenging. The lessons I learned about the importance of history, respecting diversity, engaging in different cultures, advocating for initiatives, negotiating for change, getting to know the different constituencies, and—above all—having a shared mission and strategic goals have all shaped my leadership style and initiatives.

I selected several new mentors, identified support groups, built a most incredible administrative team, and together we proceeded to lead the school. Once again, the continuous need for learning and growing is reinforced and intensified.

Through this modest journey, several themes provided my life with continuity and several goals provided my career with a sense of integration. In addition to mentorship from my grandmother, mother, father, expatriate professors, American professors and students, other themes continue to supply my leadership goals and style. Diversity, equity, globalization, and partnership are informed by my research work in women's health, theoretical work in transitions, and metatheoretical work with nursing theories and philosophies.

The bottom line is that people and interactions helped define my empowered leadership. Friends, colleagues, family, and mentees all over the world continue to inspire, challenge and support me. To all of them, I am totally indebted.

AFAF I. MELEIS, RN, PHD, FAAN, is the Margaret Bond Simon Dean of Nursing at the University of Pennsylvania (Penn) School of Nursing, professor of Nursing and Sociology, and director of the School's World Health Organization (WHO) Collaborating Center for Nursing and Midwifery Leadership. Prior to coming to Penn, she was a professor on the faculty at the University of California, Los Angeles, and the University of California, San Francisco for 34 years. She is a Fellow of the American Academy of Nursing and the College of Physicians of Philadelphia; a member of the Institute of Medicine; Trustee of the National Health Museum; and a board member of the Global Health Council and CARE, a global intervention group. She is also a board member of the Nurses Educational Funds, Inc., Life Science Career Alliance, Forum of Executive Women, and the Pennsylvania Women's Forum. She is counsel general of the International Council on Women's Health Issues (ICOWHI), an international nonprofit association dedicated to the goal of promoting health, healthcare, and well-being of women throughout the world through participation, empowerment, advocacy, education, and research. Her teaching focuses on structure and organization of nursing knowledge, transitions, health, and international nursing. Meleis' scholarship is focused on global health, immigrant and international health, women's health, and on the theoretical development of the nursing discipline. She is the author of 40 chapters, numerous monographs, proceedings, and books, and more than 150 articles in social sciences, nursing, and medical journals. Meleis is the recipient of numerous honors and awards, as well as honorary doctorates and distinguished and honorary professorships around the world. In 1990, Egyptian President Hosni Mubarak presented her the Medal of Excellence for professional and scholarly achievements. In 2000, she received the Chancellor's Medal from the University of Massachusetts, Amherst.

I have been greatly influenced in the development of this community nursing center model by the proud history of nursing, particularly the independent and innovative leaders in the areas of community health, including Lillian Wald, the mother of community health nursing."
—Sally Peck Lundeen

11

DEVELOPING AND TESTING NURSING MODELS OF CARE FOR VULNERABLE POPULATIONS

Written by Sally Peck Lundeen, RN, PhD, FAAN

My entire professional career has been spent seeking new ways to provide accessible and acceptable nursing services to inner-city communities. I attribute this directly to my graduate school experience at the University of Illinois-Chicago (UIC) medical center campus in the early 1970s. I consider myself very fortunate to have been a master's student when the psychiatric nursing curriculum shifted dramatically from a traditional, individual psychotherapeutic approach to an innovative, population-focused, community mental health approach. I was encouraged by faculty to immerse myself in communities very different than those where I had grown up. These experiences opened wonderful opportunities to meet new people, to learn from them and expand myself in so many ways. I was hooked for life!

After graduation, I worked for a number of years in community mental health settings at the height of the "movement" when federally funded mental health centers were common and nurses were part of community-based interdisciplinary teams. I was able to deliver crisis intervention, psychotherapy, and counseling services in storefront mental health centers, homes, schools, youth service agencies, and—literally—on the streets when working with troubled teens. I came to understand better the needs of families in poverty and those who were immigrants to the U.S. This period of immersion in the urban community was very important to me personally and professionally. It was during this period that I began to think about the potential to expand community-based advanced practice roles for nurses in the community.

While working in community mental health in Chicago, I decided to continue my formal education. As a doctoral student, I continued to study community-based intervention strategies and began to think about the unique skills that nurses brought to community health.

Through my work with social workers, physicians, and community health workers in the community mental health system, I began to observe significant differences in the perspectives that I brought to the team. It seemed that I was more interested in looking at things from my clients' point of view and I had difficulty separating physical health and well-being from mental health and social needs. This belief led me to tailor my interventions with troubled teens and families differently than other team members. I tended to rely more on a comprehensive assessment process and then focused on teaching as well as counseling while reframing options with clients as active participants in the process. At this point in my career, my interest in advanced practice nursing began to expand from my initial focus on mental health to include public health, primary care, and social services. I thought there must be a better way to integrate services for families in urban settings.

Erie Family Health Center, Chicago (1977-1985)

In 1976, I was asked to formally consult with social services staff on health and health-related issues emerging in clients served by a neighborhood center where I volunteered. Erie Neighborhood House in the Westtown community of Chicago had a struggling, free medical clinic staffed largely by volunteers. Soon I found myself discussing, with the neighborhood center director, the possibilities of establishing an expanded health center facility that was anchored by advanced practice nurses. In 1977, I was asked to become the Executive Director of Erie Family Health Center (EFHC), and I accepted the position for a 50% salary reduction that was all on soft money with the promise to raise the remainder of my salary as well as additional program funding for the center. EFHC became one of the nation's earliest community nursing centers. I served the EFHC community during the next eight years in spite of a move to Milwaukee, Wisconsin, that necessitated a two-hour commute each way to work, three pregnancies, and the completion of my doctoral coursework. I have often stated—ala a Peace Corps slogan—that this was "the hardest job I ever loved" and the best education for life that I could possibly have received.

During those years at EFHC, I honed my team-building skills. The staff not only represented a group with educational preparation in many different disciplines, but we also incorporated a core group of community residents as community staff members. We were quite a culturally diverse group that mirrored the transitional urban neighborhood we served. We used to laugh that an EFHC staff meeting looked like a "mini-United Nations." My greatest joy of the Erie years was the egalitarian team atmosphere that we built based on mutual respect for the multiple life experiences and world views represented by this diverse team of co-workers. This mutual respect was the basis for a style of care delivery that also respected clients as equal partners in their own healthcare.

THE LUNDEEN COMMUNITY NURSING CENTER MODEL

With the expansion of nurse practitioner programs throughout the early 1970s, nursing models of primary care delivery were surfacing in a number of states across the country as an alternative model for healthcare delivery. Although based on community models developed at the turn of the century, a definition of these modern nursing centers was proposed by an ANA Task Force upon which I served in 1987.

Nursing centers—sometimes referred to as nursing organizations, nurse-managed centers, nursing clinics, and community nursing centers—are organizations that give the client direct access to professional nursing services. Using nursing models of health, professional nurses in these centers diagnose and treat human responses to actual

and potential health problems and promote health and optimal func-
tioning among target populations and communities. The services
provided in these centers are holistic and client-centered, and are re-
imbursable at a reasonable fee level. Accountability and responsibility for client care and professional practice remain with the professional nurse. Overall accountability and responsibility remain with
the nurse executive. Nursing centers are not limited to any particular
organizational configuration. Nursing centers may be freestanding
or may be affiliated with universities or other service institutions,
such as home health agencies or hospitals. The primary characteristic of the organization is responsiveness to the health needs of the
population (Adylotte, et. al., 1987).

Although all nursing centers generally meet the criteria outlined
in the ANA definition, there are many different delivery models currently in place. Some centers provide health promotion services almost exclusively while others provide alternative models for the delivery of primary care. I have worked over the past quarter century
to develop and test a particular kind of nursing center, first at EFHC
from 1977-85 and then at the Silver Spring Community Nursing
Center in Milwaukee, Wisconsin, from 1987 to the present. I believe
that this model provides a true alternative to traditional primary
care models for vulnerable urban populations.

There continue to be a number of labels for nursing centers. Most
recently, the term "nurse-managed health centers" has been added
to the list to denote those primary care practices operated by nurses.
I have continued to stubbornly opt for the term "community nursing center" to best describe the delivery model developed at Erie and
Silver Spring, however, because I believe that there are elements that
are key to this model that are not always present in other nursing
center delivery models. The collaborative Community Nursing Center (CNC) model consciously integrates the traditional strengths of

nursing, medicine, public health, and social services while simultaneously including community residents and representatives of community organizations and institutions in a dynamic interrelationship that seeks to tailor services based on continual assessment of community needs. These CNCs provide personal care in a client-centered approach while simultaneously focusing on the health needs of specific at-risk populations and, indeed, the entire community. The CNC model is based on a vision of healthcare delivery that ensures that "comprehensive, collaborative, coordinated, culturally competent, community-based care" (Lundeen, 1993) is available to all.

CNC services are made easily accessible to community residents by providing them in convenient community-based locations where people already live, work, learn, and play. In fact, by definition, CNCs are operated *within and in partnership with* community-based social service agencies, schools, or workplaces—unlike other nursing centers that stand alone as independent practice settings. CNCs that adopt this philosophy may be sponsored by schools of nursing, comprehensive medical care systems, or not-for-profit agencies. Regardless of the organizational affiliation, an important role of the nurses in CNCs focuses on the development and maintenance of multiple collaborative partnerships. These partnerships serve to bridge the multiple and frequently fragmented service structures that exist for urban families and promote a more accessible and seamless system of care. This collaboration among service providers and community residents creates a synergy that formulates the core of the delivery model. Collaboration is the central theme of the relationships developed with other health and services providers, community residents, community agencies and organizations, funders, policy makers, and other stakeholders.

At the core of the CNC model is the integration of nursing interventions, including a strong emphasis on health promotion and

primary prevention and case management services, with those interventions traditionally provided by physicians, social workers,
and public health professionals. The CNC model also emphasizes
the need for a mix of nursing staff members that bring a variety of
expertise to the CNC setting. Clinical nurse specialists with expertise in community/ public health and mental health team with nurse
practitioners and nurse midwives to provide the range of services
to both individuals and targeted populations. In collaboration with
their colleagues from medicine, social services, and the community,
nurse experts collectively provide the link that bridges two important but very different paradigms. Nurses in CNCs play a unique
role in coordinating the efforts of physicians, counselors, social service workers, teachers, youth workers, and others on behalf of families and communities.

I have been greatly influenced in the development of this CNC
model by the proud history of nursing, particularly the independent
and innovative leaders in the areas of community health, including
Lillian Wald, the mother of community health nursing. Since the
Henry Street Settlement founded by Wald at the turn of the century,
nurses have provided care in homes, schools, and worksites. These
early nursing practices were always accessible to all community
members with an emphasis on the most disadvantaged in the community. The unique nursing roles of advocate for the most vulnerable and coordinator of health and human services are needed more
than ever today, and these early nursing center models form the
basis for the CNC models implemented at Erie and Silver Spring
Neighborhood centers.

The EFHC model focused on the development of a staff core of
master's prepared nurses, with a supporting staff of part-time physicians. About 75-80% of the primary care services were provided by
these advanced practice nurses with referrals for complex medical

problems referred to the physicians on the team. There were also social workers and community health workers on the team. In addition, we operated under the "60/40 rule" which projected that 60% of each nurse's clinician time was spent in direct primary care while the remaining 40% was spent in primary prevention and health promotion activities. In this way, we maintained the comprehensive approach that integrated primary care with public health and health promotion services. This CNC model was very well received by our clients and we expanded services significantly at the base site and opened both adolescent and senior center satellite sites during my tenure. In 1984, we were successful in securing designation as a federally funded community health center and EFHC remains a very successful community health center today.

THE COMMUNITY NURSING CENTERS AT UNIVERSITY OF WISCONSIN-MILWAUKEE (1987-PRESENT)

I left Erie Family Health Center in 1985 to join the faculty at University of Wisconsin-Milwaukee (UWM) College of Nursing. The seven years of commuting the 90 miles to Chicago on an almost daily basis were taking a toll, and I was about to deliver our third child. My husband (who had been amazingly supportive during this long tenure at Erie) and I decided it was time for me to work in Milwaukee, where we lived. I was thrilled to accept a position at UWM where one of the earliest academic nursing centers had been established in 1979. I was soon appointed UWM nursing center director and sought to expand the campus-based services into the community. I had the support of Dean Norma Lang at UWM to undertake this expansion, with the clear understanding that I would have to find extramural revenue streams to support it.

After a number of interviews with social service organization directors in 1986, I discovered the Silver Spring Neighborhood Center (SSNC) on Milwaukees's northwest side. This 25-year-old agency provided a very broad scope of educational, recreational, and social support services, but it did not have a healthcare component. I explained the CNC model first to the director and then to the community board. I knew that I had found the right organizational partner when someone asked, "Why haven't we done this before?" In January, 1987, I secured a small, private grant from the Cudahy Foundation and opened a drop-in nursing center at SSNC several mornings a week—in a repainted janitorial closet. That spring, I began a full community assessment with the help of the students in a graduate community health course that I was teaching. That assessment became the core of a proposal to the United States Department of Health and Human Services Health Resources and Service Administration (HRSA), and we received three-year funding in the fall of 1987 from the HRSA's Division of Nursing as one of the first federally funded academic nursing centers. Faculty colleagues followed with other CNCs sponsored by UWM's College of Nursing at a homeless shelter in Kenosha, Wisconsin (Shalom CNC, established in 1990); a social service agency in Milwaukee (House of Peace CNC, established 1991); and, an elementary school in Milwaukee (Riverwest Pierce CNC, established 1996).

In 1996, I founded the UWM Institute for Urban Health Partnerships (IUHP) to serve as the administrative unit for the practice activities of the college. Today the IUHP serves as the UWM College of Nursing organizational umbrella for all the community nursing centers, faculty practice activities, and contracts related to community-based initiatives.

THE NEED TO DOCUMENT NURSING PRACTICE AND THE IMPACT ON VULNERABLE URBAN POPULATIONS

I had only one regret when I left Erie Family Health Center: Although there was abundant anecdotal evidence that the CNC model was an excellent way to deliver care, I had no data that could specifically document what the nurse clinicians' interventions had been nor the relationship of these nurse interventions to client outcomes. Although the EFHC team had implemented a highly successful and innovative CNC model that led to transformational change in the populations we served, we had not collected data elements that we served. I swore to myself that I would never make that mistake again.

Soon after establishing SSNC, my team and I began searching for a computerized clinical information system that would allow us to document our nursing practice and link nursing interventions to client outcomes. We wanted a software program that was affordable; captured clinical as well as financial and billing data; and documented nursing practice, including health promotion and case management activities, and both group and individual primary clinical care. We wanted this information system to result in a relational database that would support health services and outcomes research as well as the more standard administrative and clinical applications. We insisted that in addition to standard medical terminology collected in primary care settings, we needed to collect standardized nursing terminology so as to measure the impact of nursing practice. We could find no product on the market that met these criteria.

In 1987, with the assistance of a very skilled computer programmer who volunteered his time, we began to develop our own system. Automated Community Health Information System (ACHIS) was implemented at SSNC in October 1988. This clinical information system has been through many upgrades and currently operates on a web-based platform that can accommodate clinical data at multiple sites. Point of service entry was initiated in the upgraded software release in spring 2005. A centralized data repository allows storage and retrieval of a relational clinical dataset for analysis by the UWM IUHP research team. We are using this data set as the basis for a program of longitudinal research that seeks new knowledge about the nature of the urban populations served and their utilization patterns, nursing practice in a CNC, and the relationship of nurse interventions to client outcomes and costs of care.

The integration of standardized nursing terminology into clinical information systems has subsequently become another research focus that has intersected with and complemented my focus on the implementation and testing of CNC models of care. I have been continually amazed and frustrated that, despite substantial anecdotal evidence that nurses provide unique and significant contributions to the improved health status of many populations, specific nursing data remain essentially invisible in the data collected and used for quality assurance, research, and policy decisions. I continue to believe that the ability to describe specific nursing interventions and link them to the outcomes of various populations is an essential step in making changes in healthcare delivery and policy. In order to determine the potential of nursing models of care, researchers must identify sufficiently large CNC client populations. Given the limited number of clients served by typical nursing centers, multiple site studies are essential. Clinical information systems that collect standardized nursing data will be critical to conduct these multiple site studies.

In 2001, a proposal to the USDHHS' Agency for Healthcare Research and Quality (AHRQ) to support the implementation of the Nursing Center Research Network (NCRN) was funded. The NCRN is comprised of 20 academic nursing centers affiliated with 17 research-intensive universities located in 13 states. It is one of only two federally funded nursing primary care research networks of nurses in the nation. One of the NCRN objectives is to establish computerized clinical information systems in a number of nursing centers that will support the collection of standardized nursing data across settings. I continue to be optimistic that studies using the resulting database will contribute to the development of knowledge about the potential of nurses to improve health outcomes for vulnerable populations in many community settings. I look forward to working with colleagues through the NCRN to establish one of the first clinical data repositories capable of health services and nursing outcomes research using nursing clinical data elements.

LESSONS LEARNED

When I assess the lessons learned in my professional journey, I can summarize very briefly:

1. **Follow your passion:** Life is too short to invest significant energy on issues that are not important to you.

2. **Be patient and persistent:** Never give up. Transformational change takes time and may require intense focus on the goal.

3. **Collaborate, collaborate, collaborate:** You can nearly always accomplish more and assure greater impact when you partner with others.

4. **Don't think scrawny:** Make sure your goals are big enough to be worthy of your investment.

It has been my honor and privilege to work with some of the most dedicated, innovative, and skilled community nurses in the nation. I have learned so much from them. We have all learned even more from the individuals and families that we have served together. The opportunity to develop and test nursing center models that have the potential to improve the health status of vulnerable populations has been my passion. This professional work has been a joy and a privilege. I hope to continue to partner with colleagues from across the country to seek the evidence necessary to support real health policy changes on their behalf.

SALLY PECK LUNDEEN, RN, PhD, FAAN, has focused her entire professional career on the implementation and evaluation of community based nursing practice models in vulnerable urban communities. She has undertaken this work in both academic and practice settings in Illinois and Wisconsin. As executive director of the Erie Family Health Center (1977-1985) she expanded a part-time "free clinic" in a Hispanic community in Chicago to a multiple site federally funded community health center which continues to flourish today. Her appointment as a faculty member at the University of Wisconsin-Milwaukee (UWM) moved this work into the academic nursing center arena. At UWM, she developed and supervises four community nursing centers and was the founder and first director of the UWM Institute for Urban Health Partnerships. She served as the associate dean for practice and interim dean before her appointment in 2001 as dean of the School of Nursing. Lundeen's research and publications have focused on community nursing centers, computerized clinical documentation for community nursing practice, transformational leadership, and health policy. She is passionate about professional nursing and improving the health status of vulnerable urban populations. Dr. Lundeen has been the recipient of numerous awards from consumer groups as well as professional organizations, including a Primary Care Public Policy Fellowship from Health Resources and Services Administration, the National League for Nursing's Lavinia Dock Award, the Wisconsin Governor's Primary Health Care Educator Award, the 2000 Milwaukee Business Journal Woman of Influence Award, the MDNA 2002 Service Award for Excellence in Nursing Management and Administration, and the National Nursing Centers Consortium 2004 Champion Award for her pioneering leadership of the nurse-managed health center movement. She was most recently elected first board chair of the recently-established Wisconsin Center for Nursing.

*It is a false statement that only rocket scientists
can create a strategic plan.*
—Salvatore J. Tagliareni

12

IT DOES NOT MATTER
WHICH WAY YOU GO

Written by Salvatore J. Tagliareni, PhD

There is a wonderful moment in *Alice's Adventures in Wonderland* by Lewis Carroll when Alice has a choice to make about direction. She asks the Cheshire Cat which direction she should take. There are two roads, and the question is: "Which road should I take?" This question is met with another response from the Cheshire Cat: "That depends a good deal on where you want to get to." Alice replied, "I don't much care where." And the cat answered, "Then it doesn't matter which way you go."

This simple example points out the need for planning and creating direction which is the most significant purpose of strategic planning. It is a process that helps the organization or group focus on where it wants to go over a specific time period and how it intends to get there. It is the process of involving the entire organization or group in developing the road map that will be followed.

WHAT STRATEGIC PLANNING IS <u>NOT</u>

- A crystal ball that predicts the future;

- A plan that understands completely in advance all the major issues that will challenge the organization;

- A concrete, static document that will undergo no change or alteration during the plan's time limit;

- A plan developed in isolation from the rest of the organization;

- A document that we develop and then ignore until the next planning process.

WHAT STRATEGIC PLANNING <u>IS</u>

- An organized attempt to clearly define the purpose and vision of the organization;

- A process of communication for the entire organization;

- A method to involve all of the stakeholders;

- A way to focus on strategies not merely activities;

- A backdrop for critical decision making;

- A basis for evaluation of goals and adjustment opportunities;

- A process to establish key goals and provide goal alignment;

- A way to assess the best allocation of resources;

- An ideal way to develop people and provide leadership opportunities;

- A process to create an ideal that is larger than individual achievements or goals.

It is important, before we describe the planning process, for the reader to understand some of my bias points.

Sal's Bias Points

- It is a false statement that only rocket scientists can create a strategic plan.

- It is a false statement that perfect resources must be present to create an effective plan.

- It is a false statement that the organization must go on hold until the plan is fully completed.

- It is a false statement that nurses do not have the capability or experience to develop an effective plan.

- It is a true statement that strategic planning requires the full commitment of senior leadership.

- It is a true statement that the message be consistent that the organization is serious about this plan.

- It is a true statement that all members of the organization need to be involved in the plan.

- It is a true statement that the leadership makes it clear that this plan is not merely a management fad.

- It is a true statement that the plan requires that we look at all the sacred cows that we believe are untouchable and unchangeable.

- It is a true statement that there is always resistance to the plan and we should take it seriously.

- It is a true statement that people will only change when the changes create achievements that cannot be met solely by individual performances.

- It is a true statement that without the focus of a plan the organization tends to spend its energy on activities and not strategy.

- It is a true statement that without a plan people gravitate toward doing what they know best and not necessarily what is best for the organization.

THE PLANNING PROCESS

Creating the Vision for the Organization

Most organizations are so caught up in daily activities and crises that there is never a sense of where the organization is headed. Often there are jokes or comments about the craziness of the organization and the hectic pace that never seems to allow the opportunity to pause and reflect. The concept of a plan becomes ludicrous, and the next flurry of demands and activities take all our energy and attention. This state of affairs often leads to burnout. At the end of a stressful day or period of time we walk away without a sense of accomplishment. Though we know we make a difference, the situation becomes draining. It is hard to find energy and inspiration when this is the constant norm. There seems no time to define our purpose or to look at bigger issues. The needs mount and the idea of having a plan seems purely academic. The difficulty with this all too common set of circumstances is that it will not get better without focus and a method to make decisions on a different set of opportunities. "Busy up to our eyes" in things that should be done will always be present, but where are we going? What are we trying to accomplish together? What would this place be and how would it function if we had the magic wand? We would like to take the time and energy to invest in these questions, but do they seem like pie in the sky time? We would like to find a better way but feel powerless to start the process.

The Process Begins With Establishing the Vision for the Organization

- What do you want this organization to look like a year from now?

- What should be our focus?

- If we had reasonable resources what could we achieve?

- What should we value?

- What will finished look like?

- What would it be like if we did not have the current problems and constraints?

- What terrific goals could we achieve in the next year?

- If we stretched the organization what could we achieve?

121

- What would we like our clients and stakeholders to say about us a year from now?

Do Not Be Hung Up on the Word "Realistic" at This Time

We are not at the stage where we are allocating resources. The word "realistic" often stifles creativity and we create a vision that is mediocre at best. This is an opportunity to freely look at the potential organization that we desire. It is the view that will provide ENERGY and INSPIRATION. People will buy into something significant rather than a tweak of what they already know.

It has been my experience that an organization can move light years when the vision has understanding and acceptance by the stakeholders.

Write down your vision as tightly and succinctly as possible and have the stakeholders review and give input. Stakeholders are any persons or groups that will be affected by the success or failure of your plan. What would you like the stakeholders to say about your organization a year from now? Be as specific as possible. What would they say about you today? How do you know that and what are your communication methods that verify this? What is the data that indicates the current status? One way to get at this is to do an environmental survey of all the pluses and minuses that support or detract from what you want them to say about you a year from now.

Example:
We would like the nursing staff to say they feel they are valued and appreciated by the administration.

What are the things in place that support this outcome? What concrete processes are in place to indicate we are on target? What is their current feedback? What are the biggest challenges to achieve this? What are the obstacles in current practices or past history? What are we willing to do to achieve this? What are we no longer willing to do to achieve this? What are the resources we will need to do this? Who should be the leader or leaders in heading this up?

We need to really understand how close or far we are from the desired outcome and this takes a gut-level honesty. This is the process of refining the data, and as the plan goes on we will see that the vision which initially seems like purely an ideal becomes more real as we follow the plan through the eyes of the stakeholders. As we assess the pluses and minuses of the data, it will lead us to areas that will help develop the strategies.

Looking at what we want the nurses to say about the organization a year from now we need to define the following: What is our goal in this area? What do we wish to achieve in a year? This should be as specific as possible and have some measurement indicators. Remember we are not at the stage of allocating resources yet, and we have work to do before that happens, but we are refining as we go, and we are learning about our organization. One of the benefits of the process is that the planning group sees the whole organization, not just their part. A helpful method in looking at the critical goals of the organization and stakeholders is to look at each goal through the eyes of these questions:

- Do we reflect values that support this goal? For example, do we assist our nursing staff in their pursuit of excellent service?
  - Do we develop their skills and involve them in key decisions?
  - Do they receive feedback on a regular basis?
  - Are we supportive in the way we communicate the key goals of the organization?

- Do we have the right people in the right jobs?
  - Have we prepared them for the changes and challenges they face?
  - How do we upgrade their skills and provide training and development?
  - Are they aware of the key strategies and goals of the organization?
  - Do they understand their part in achieving these?
  - Do they have reasonable resources to achieve these?
- What is the style of current management?
  - Is it conducive to the achievement of these goals?
  - How do we guide them through the necessary changes and what have we done to understand their resistance or confusion about the changes?

This Process Should Be Repeated for Every Group of Stakeholders

Some of these would include administrators, clients, other departments and organizations, etc.

WHERE ARE WE NOW?

- We have established a view of the desired organization a year from now.
- We have arrived at this by involving all of the stakeholders.
- We have defined what we want them to say about us a year from now.
- We have examined their current view of the stakeholders.
- We have defined what we must add and delete to achieve the desired outcomes.

- We have a rough estimate of what it will take in the area of resources.
- We have a better understanding of the whole organization.
- We are moving toward strategy rather than merely activities.
- We are laying the groundwork for how we allocate our resources.
- We are seeing what we value and how we must model these values.
- We are developing the entire staff through the process.

THE NEXT STEPS

Select a major goal for all of the stakeholders and have leadership rank them in order of preference.

- Which can be achieved in the period of a year?
- Which ones contribute significantly to the achievement of the vision?
- Which ones do we have the reasonable resources to achieve?
- How will we measure progress and how will we adjust to unforeseen changes?
- Share these with the entire organization and work feedback into the plan.

HOW TO GET STARTED:

Leadership should begin by (if possible) holding an off-site two-day planning meeting. If resources allow, hire a planner or facilitator to initiate the process. All of the first parts of the plan—the structure of a vision, the identification of the stakeholders, and an environmental assessment—are reasonable achievements at the end of the two days.

All departments should be represented at the meeting and communications with the entire organization and all stakeholders should be sent before the meeting. The outcomes and next steps should be communicated to all as soon as possible. Follow-up sessions and timelines should be defined by the end of the meeting.

Closing Guidelines

- Resist the temptation to do the *Operational Plan* instead of the *Strategic Plan*. You don't want activities only: You desire the achievement of a *VISION* through goals and strategies.

- Listen to all the stakeholders—not just the defined leaders.

- Do not get hung up on the details at this stage.

- Don't put the plan in a drawer and ignore it; make it the driving force of the organization.

- Don't canonize the plan; changes will have to be made as you develop the implementation.

SALVATORE J.TAGLIARENI, PhD, has been an organizational development consultant for more than 25 years. He has consulted for multinational corporations, including Johnson & Johnson, Hoffman LaRoche, Bristol Meyers Squibb, IBM, and a host of other Fortune 1000 companies. He is the author of *The Musings of a Pilgrim*. Tagliareni is the founder of Next Step Associates. Together with Dr.Luigi Contini, he developed a strategic planning methodology that focuses on vision, organizational empowerment, and process engineering. He receieved his PhD from the International University in 1973 in human behavior and leadership. He is currently a principal in Tagliareni Anderson Fine Art and operates an art gallery featuring 19th- and 20th-century American art.

IV

LEADERSHIP IS ... INTENTIONAL

Life is a bunch of trade-offs. By the end of the day, you will not be able to accomplish every-thing you may have hoped or dreamed, but if you are true to yourself, you will feel good about your choices and the trade-offs you had to make."

—Jane Eisner

13

MANAGING YOUR CAREER: AN INTERVIEW WITH JANE EISNER

Written by Tine Hansen-Turton, BA, MGA, JD

"I had a deep interest in journalism since junior high school, where I focused on writing, reporting, and formulating ideas and critical thinking. At college, where I studied English in a liberal arts program, I was the first woman editor of our college newspaper. It just happened that I was at the right place at the right time, which enabled me to move into the editor position."

After college, Jane Eisner worked for a few smaller newspapers. She quickly went back to school and got her master's in journalism from Columbia University. After she graduated, she moved to Norfolk, Virginia, to write for the local paper. Originally from New York, she wanted to get away from the big city. Norfolk was the perfect small community to do so. In 1980, Jane married her husband, and they moved to Philadelphia. She was only 24, but she got a job right away at the *Philadelphia Inquirer*. She was the youngest person ever hired there. Her first assignment was to cover the suburban section of the paper.

Lesson 1: Compromise is Everything

"When my husband got a job in Philadelphia, I was petrified of change and changing my job. We were young and we did not have much security. But what I have since learned is that if you put priorities in place, the right things will happen to you in your life. A good marriage is key."

When Jane later got a two-year assignment as a foreign correspondent in London, another compromise was made. She moved to London with their small child, and her husband joined her six months later after getting a fellowship. Later, she went into editing, where she spent 10 years, followed by 10 years of management. In 1990, she became the assistant to the editor, which started her upper management track and ultimately landed her the job as editor-in-chief.

LESSON 2: YOU CAN RISE TO THE TOP TOO QUICKLY AND LOSE YOURSELF ON YOUR JOURNEY

"I came up too fast at the *Philadelphia Inquirer*. I did not realize all that was going on. I was too consumed with it all. My initial goal was to run a newspaper, and I was on the right track. My career path was wonderful, but controlled by someone else—a man."

By 1999, while Jane was at the top of her game, she was burning out and had to ask herself, "What is it that I really want to do?"

"You should not be doing work if your heart is not with the program. My goal changed along the way, as your family impacts your choices. Many people move around in journalism but I had a family, a life, and moving from city to city is not what is always good for a family "

So much of Jane's career had been dictated by what a successful newspaper editor does, which is to ultimately be the managing editor and run the paper. But Jane was not interested in being in charge. She loved her job on the editorial board but she also needed family time.

LESSON 3: THINK OF YOUR LIFE IN STAGES

"I think of life in stages. After a year of a lot of searching, I followed my heart's desire. I wanted to write a book, write and teach."

In 1999, Jane stepped down from the editorial board. She got a fellowship to study at the University of Pennsylvania. Jane began writing her own column in 2000 for the *Philadelphia Inquirer*, which currently appears on Thursdays. She also teaches part-time at the Fox Leadership program. She wrote a book, *Taking Back the Vote, Getting American Youth Involved in Democracy*. She feels strongly about involving youth in democracy. The book's publication was very timely, appearing just before the 2004 presidential election.

Lesson 4: Mentors are Like Mirrors—They Enable You to See How the World Perceives You

Max King, who was the editor from 1990-1997, was Jane's mentor. He initially asked her to be his assistant and then he put her in different jobs over the years.

"I missed not being mentored by Max in my later years at the *Inquirer*. Mentors are key; they are always thinking a step or two ahead of you. The higher up you go on the professional ladder, the harder it is to find mentors. It gets lonely at the top. I was really disappointed that there were not any female mentors at the *Inquirer*."

Jane has had a lot of unofficial mentors, such as friends who are women. As a woman, Jane feels she has a responsibility to give back something, so she mentors several female reporters.

"Mentors are like mirrors, which enable you to see how other people perceive you. How you are perceived is critical to your success. You need someone to be honest and give you constructive criticism."

Lesson 5: A paper is an Ongoing Communication

Women have traditionally not been good at engaging journalists for stories. But, they are getting better. Jane encourages people to get to know journalists and editors. It is all about relationships. Get to know reporters and over time they will trust you and use you as a source.

"Know the players, cultivate the people, read the paper, see who is writing what. A paper is an ongoing communication, trafficking ideas."

The people she goes back to are accessible, have interesting things to say, are not stingy and are, in general, interesting people.

Lesson 6: Take ownership of your own life

"I have done a lot of soul searching. I always blamed work for personal failings and frustrations, but what I have learned is that we all need to take ownership of our own lives. What do you want out of life? How do you learn to compromise and not blame other people and your family for not obtaining all that you want? I used to be late— always blaming others for my lateness—even though I was the one with the problem. I don't do that anymore. Life is a bunch of trade-offs. By the end of the day, you will not be able to accomplish everything you may have hoped or dreamed, but if you are true to yourself, you will feel good about your choices and the trade-offs you had to make."

JANE EISNER, a pioneer in Philadelphia journalism, joined the National Constitution Center as vice president for Civic Initiatives in January 2006 after serving in various leadership positions at *The Philadelphia Inquirer* for more than 25 years. She creates and manages programs to further expand the National Constitution Center's presence as a leader in national civic education and engagement. She is responsible for the Center's flagship Constitution Day programs and events, as well as The Peter Jennings Institution for Journalism and the Constitution and an annual Constitutional Convention, a signature initiative to engage young people from around the country in deliberation and debate about the values and relevance of the United States Constitution. Before joining the Constitution Center, Eisner was a familiar face and voice at *The Philadelphia Inquirer* where she served as a reporter, city hall bureau chief, and foreign correspondent before becoming editorial page editor in 1994. She began writing her nationally-syndicated column, "American Rhythms," in 2000. She is the author of *Taking Back the Vote: Getting American Youth Involved in our Democracy*, published in 2004, and her work has appeared in major national publications. She is a senior fellow at the Robert A. Fox Leadership Program at the University of Pennsylvania where she teaches in the political science and critical writing departments. Eisner is actively involved in the community, serving as president of the Pennsylvania Women's Forum, Trustee and Secretary of The Philadelphia Award, and a mentor for Philadelphia Futures, among other roles. She is a graduate of Wesleyan University and received her master's degree from Columbia University School of Journalism. She lives in Merion with her husband, Dr. Mark Berger, and their three children.

While you still need to attend the big fundraisers, all politics is truly local. Anyone can walk into a legislator's office and meet the staffers.
—Colleen Conway-Welch, RN, PhD, FAAN

14

ALL BUSINESS: LESSONS LEARNED FROM AN INTERVIEW WITH COLLEEN CONWAY-WELCH

Written by Tine Hansen-Turton, BA, MGA, JD

I first met Dr. Colleen Conway-Welch a few years ago at a Tufts University conference on health. She was a speaker, the lone nurse among a room full of doctors. In my experience, I have found that physicians frequently do not engage with nurse speakers. However, as Colleen addressed the physician audience, she captured everyone with her humor, charm, and relentless energy. I, for one, was hooked.

Colleen has a broad array of national connections in well-placed political settings. I had heard incredible things about her as the longest-serving dean of the Vanderbilt University School of Nursing. A mentor of mine, Arlene, once told me, "You are only two phone calls away from the U.S. President." I did not believe her, but I have since come to realize that she is close to the truth. Colleen is one of these people who truly *is* just a few calls away from the president. She has the kind of political access a political "wannabe" like me could only dream of. When you talk to her, she consistently brings strategy and positioning to the forefront.

Colleen knew early on that she wanted to go places in life. She set her eye on corporate boards. She always had a goal in mind and has consistently achieved those goals. She sits on numerous corporate boards, including for a bank.

COLLEEN'S LESSONS

Get where the action is. Political fundraisers are not just for the rich and famous. If you cannot afford to go to four or five-figure receptions and dinners, find a way to work at them—collect the money or register guests—so you can still be there. In the nursing field this is a big issue. Despite being the largest U.S. healthcare profession, nurses are still not acknowledged as partners by many of their medical and political counterparts. Part of this is due to nurses not being present at large fundraisers where presence means everything.

Know when it is time to cut your losses and let go. This is a lesson few want to accept. People have a hard time letting go of a person or an idea if they have a personal investment in it.

All politics are truly local—so spend your time there. While you still need to attend the big fundraisers, all politics are truly local. Anyone can walk into a legislator's office and meet the staffers. Having spent a few years advocating on Capitol Hill, I know the importance of getting to know the young 20-something staffers. She or he just graduated from a top college with some general knowledge and is now serving a congressperson in a very responsible position. Most of them have little knowledge about the intricacies of the issues with which they are being presented from savvy lobbyists, but they have no choice but to learn what they can.

Make friends with financial people. You have to have relevance to your institution or organization—look at how you can fill other departments' and stakeholders' needs.

Finally, **package everything you do—and everything your organization does—well and with a high level of sensitivity toward what your audience wants to hear.**

COLLEEN CONWAY-WELCH, RN, PhD, FAAN, has served as professor and dean of Vanderbilt University School of Nursing since 1984. She has been active in nursing practice and nursing education for more than 30 years. The holder of three honorary doctorates from Cumberland University, Georgetown University, and the University of Colorado, she is a graduate of Georgetown University, Catholic University of America, and New York University. She has published extensively, served on President Reagan's Commission on the HIV Epidemic in 1988, the National Bipartisan Commission on the Future of Medicare in 1998, the Governor's Tennessee Commission on the Future of TennCare, was appointed by Secretary of Homeland Security Tommy Thompson to the Secretary's Council on Public Health Preparedness, Office of the Assistant Secretary for Public Health Emergency Preparedness, DHHS. She is a member of the Medicare Coverage Advisory Committee (MCAC) with the Department of Health & Human Services and is a member of the George Washington University Homeland Security Policy Institute. She is a fellow in the American Academy of Nursing, a charter fellow of the American College of Nurse-Midwives, a member of the Institute of Medicine and serves as a director on the boards of Pinnacle Bank, Rehab Care Group, Caremark Rx, Inc., and Ardent Health Services. She is the founding director of the International Nursing Coalition for Mass Casualty Education, Inc, Ardent Health Services, and chairs the Nurse Advisory Committee for Health Stream, Inc.

Someone smart once said that if you cannot make a professional impression on a 20-second elevator ride, you will be less successful than those that can.
—Tine Hansen-Turton

15

THE ELEVATOR RIDE PITCH AND OTHER LEADERSHIP TIDBITS

Written by Tine Hansen-Turton, BA, MGA, JD

STRATEGY AND ACTION

Someone smart once said that if you cannot make a professional impression on a 20-second elevator ride, you will be less successful than those that can. The idea is that you should be able to tell a person, in 20 seconds or less, about the role of your company and why it is relevant to that person. This sounds a lot easier than it really is. The concept, however, is great, and I admit that on more than one occasion I have ridden an elevator up and down just to catch the attention of someone important.

If you need to get in touch with a high-ranking official in a government agency or company, spend some time in the building they reside in professionally. The events of September 11, 2001, have made this strategy harder to carry out. The first time I tried this strategy was when I was working for housing and wanted to get the attention of the U.S. Housing and Urban Development (HUD) secretary at that time to talk about important healthcare initiatives. I happened to be in Washington, DC, for a meeting held in the HUD building. So, I decided to ride the elevator up to the secretarial floor just in case I might catch him. Unbelievably, I get up there and see the secretary preparing to get in a different elevator, so I jumped out and jumped into his elevator. My 20-second spiel had been prepared, and I piqued his interest enough to obtain contact with his key deputy on the issue.

ON POLICY AND POLITICS: WHY WE ALL MUST BE ENGAGED

If you want to make a change in the world, one way of doing it is to become involved in politics. Do it by yourself or through your professional associations. It helps to have money, but it isn't necessary.

Here is my "Top 10" list of the basics for getting involved. All of these tips go back to one premise, espoused by President Lyndon B. Johnson, "It is not who you know; it's who you get to know."

1. Become familiar with the political process—it is a dance that requires persistence and patience.

2. Get to know your legislators, if you can. Even better, get to know their staff at the local, state, and federal levels.

3. Learn all you can about your local, state, and federal agencies that deal with healthcare credentialing, licensing, and healthcare funding. Remember, they can make or break you.

4. Establish relationships with legislators, legislative staff, health commissioners, and local, state, and federal key staff members and department heads—it's all about who you know.

5. Don't shy away from using your relationships when necessary—in politics everything is *quid pro quo.*

6. Become a resource of knowledge for staff in both the executive and legislative branches. You are the expert in your own field, and they will respect your opinion.

7. Develop broad-based support for your issue; use students, patients, and the community you work in.

8. Place key financial political supporters on your board of directors and/or trustees if you are in a leadership position.

9. Feed information about healthcare issues to staffers near and dear to you, as often as you can. There is an old saying that if you put the issue in front of elected or appointed officials, eventually they will own it.

10. Remember: the political process is a dance, so don't get comfortable when you are successful in changing a regulation,

getting better reimbursement, and being a good advocate for your patient. Enemies are always lurking, waiting to undo what you just successfully achieved!

(See page VI for biographical profile.)

"Success is all about using and getting used, and knowing when both
are happening."
—Susan Sherman, RN, MA

16

MENTORS AND MENTEES:
AN INTERVIEW WITH
SUSAN SHERMAN

Written by Tine Hansen-Turton, BA, MGA, JD

Susan Sherman has been my mentor for nearly a decade. She is one of the few people I know willing and able to mentor a number of people at the same time and to take the time to support them. I owe a lot of gratitude to what she did to position me as a leader in the local community, and she has inspired me to continue the path of mentoring those who work with me.

Susan wanted to be a nurse from an early age. She grew up in an educated household where her parents and grandparents had gone to college. Nursing was the career that was made for her. "Nurses are unique problem solvers and leaders in their own rights. It is one of the most respected professions."

"Life is Logical. You Structure and Plan It, But It Is Also Serendipitous. Those Moments Are Available to Everyone."

While Susan was the chair at Community College of Philadelphia, an old friend and mentor called her up one day and requested that she come to lunch at the Union League. The Union League, until a decade ago, was an exclusive men's club. Women had to enter through the back door with the employees.

When Susan arrived at the lunch table, her mentor had brought three older men with him. None of them spoke, except her respected mentor, who proceeded to interview her for a job she had not known existed. She was being interviewed for a board seat with the Independence Foundation. It's been reported to her that when she left the table one of the gentlemen said, "She is young, so she will live a long time on the board."

Susan Sherman joined the board of the Independence Foundation in May 1993. At that time, the Independence Foundation had no professional staff, no programs, and no direction for the board. So,

over the next two years, Susan prepared for the job she wanted
to get.

Susan's father always told her, "You get the job you have been doing." So, she worked hard as a volunteer on the board. During weekends and evenings, she would review grant proposals, write guidelines
and work on the overall direction of the foundation. Eventually the
other board members realized they needed a staff and a leader, and
Susan was the choice. After all, she had been doing the job already.

I first met Susan in 1995, when she had just taken over as the
president and CEO of the Independence Foundation. John White,
my boss at the Philadelphia Housing Authority at the time, had returned from lunch with a scribbled note to me to follow-up with
Susan regarding some of the work we were doing to bring healthcare
to our public housing population. I was very busy at the time, but I
knew that following up with contacts can be career making or break-
ing. So, I called her and we made plans to meet at her offices on the
penthouse level of a very old building. It took two elevators to get
there—a set of modern elevators and then a small, antique looking
elevator with manual gates and sliding doors. Susan met me with
welcoming arms, and we sat down and talked about public housing.
She had numerous questions. Little did I know that I was being interviewed for my future position as director of what is now the National
Nursing Centers Consortium. We bonded, and she put me in touch
with nursing schools and advanced practice nurses who could help in
my efforts to bring quality care to Philadelphia-area housing populations. Our dialogue that day would eventually lead me down the path
of working with nurse-managed health centers and include me in this
amazing movement that continues to grow and grow.

Fortunately, Susan was always good at finding mentors to help
her with the next step in her career. When asked about what are the

qualifications of a good mentee, Susan says, "They ask to be mentored." Further, it has to be a relationship built on trust, not just teaching and learning. "Success is all about using and getting used, and knowing when both are happening."

Susan's philosophy is predicated on surrounding herself with bright people. "The more success they have, the more you have as a leader." Susan has always been good at utilizing friends and receiving support. She established her own inner circle when she became the president of the Independence Foundation because she wanted a group of honest friends who would tell her if she was stepping out of line, a kind of kitchen cabinet. The kitchen cabinet members serve as the true mirror that reaches out with honesty and pulls you back. For her, being a leader of a foundation is not easy. The hardest job, she says, is saying "no" to good ideas and programs and staying true to her mission.

Finally, Susan taught me that people are not expendable. There is a notion in the private sector to the contrary, but reality is otherwise. If you are in a leadership position and leave your post, you will undoubtedly also leave an indelible mark on that organization.

Since Susan took over the foundation with her effective board team, the Independence Foundation has become one of the most influential foundations in the area. They are very visible and respected in the greater Philadelphia region and have been recognized locally and nationally for what they have done to position nursing professionals as the leaders in healthcare delivery.

(See page VII for biographical profile.)

146

V

LEADERSHIP IS ... TRANSFORMATIVE

17

A Leader is One Who Knows the Way ... Goes the Way ... and Shows the Way: An Interview with Dr. Gloria Smith

Written by Vernice Ferguson, RN, MA, FAAN, FRCN

My conversation with Dr. Smith reinforced the truism that, "A leader is one who knows the way... Goes the way... and Shows the way." In preparation for the interview, Dr. Smith was asked to think about the following:

- What are some of the defining experiences on the way to the top that contributed to your success as an international nursing leader?

- Was your rise to prominence planned methodically or did opportunities present themselves?

- What are some of the lessons that you learned along the way that others can benefit from?

The Early Years

Dr. Smith's early years were spent in Detroit. Her family migrated there from the southern United States. Her nursing preparation was acquired at Wayne (Wayne became Wayne State in 1956), from which she graduated in 1955. Upon graduation, her first position—which she loved—was with the Visiting Nurse Association (VNA) of Detroit. While an undergraduate student, she worked as a "contingent nurse" at VNA on weekends. As a junior nursing student, she had a clinical practicum at the VNA. She never sought her first position; instead, the VNA sought her. She worked there from 1955 to 1963. She will tell you that in the 1950s, nurses were in charge. Interdisciplinary practice was in place. "People respected each other's practice." Home care was in place with case conferences and team care evident.

She was recruited to Tuskegee Institute (now known as Tuskegee University, a school founded by Booker T. Washington). Her knowledge of public health nursing was sought by Dr. Lillian Harvey, a pioneering leader in nursing education, to develop the public health segment of the curriculum in the accredited school of nursing for blacks. In less than six months in operation, the program was accredited. Dr. Smith did not, however, find a nurturing environment there.

On leaving Tuskegee she joined her husband, who was in the military and stationed in Georgia. She taught at Albany State University. Following the Georgia teaching experience, Dr. Smith first worked as a district supervisor and nurse consultant for the Oklahoma Health Department and then became the dean of the University of Oklahoma School of Nursing, where she served for 10 years. During her tenure at Oklahoma, she was able to procure a new building for the school and developed a continuing education program, a nurse practitioner certificate program, and a master's degree program.

THE RETURN TO MICHIGAN

Dr. Smith returned to her home state of Michigan to become the first nurse to head the Department of Public Health for the state of Michigan. While serving as state health director, she succeeded in distributing funds where they were needed, a success not achieved easily in government agencies. In 1988, she returned to her alma mater, Wayne State University, and served as dean of the School of Nursing for three years. In 1991, she went to the W.K. Kellogg Foundation to coordinate their health programming and was promoted to vice president in 1995. She retired from Kellogg in 2002.

At the W.K. Kellogg Foundation and beyond, Dr. Smith was well known for her pioneering work in community-based programs. She helped communities find their voice. She loved her international work and made a lasting contribution across southern Africa as she worked with nurses and other healthcare officials to assure better educated nurse leaders were prepared academically in their own regions for advanced practice and leadership. Dr. Smith traveled tirelessly and extensively to South Africa, before and after apartheid, and takes great pride in the increased number of doctorally prepared nurses.

REMINISCENCES

When queried regarding her personal rise to leadership in a remarkable and eclectic career, she will tell you that it was not planned methodically, that it was planned no more than wanting to rise in the nursing profession. She stated, "I always felt that I was a leader." Early on she identified the practice of nursing as essential and that she was in charge of nursing from "day one" with patients and their families. She recalled that her clinical education was different than that of today. As she practiced nursing, she found fulfillment at every level. "So many things gave me pleasure. I was pleased with myself and my peers for we did significant work." As she spoke she lamented the power and potential of our practice being missed. "Nurses are not leading where they can lead. That's what it is all about. So many interventions could take place that are not occurring."

For a while she spoke of her socialization, and that of her classmates, into nursing. There were mandatory teas and opportunities to attend musical plays. The underlying philosophy was that you must develop as a whole person. She remains grateful for her basic nursing education experience. She learned so much. There were good mentors and role models all within a nurturing environment and with the personal involvement of the faculty.

On her rise to leadership and throughout her prestigious career, Dr. Smith will tell you that she cannot relate to being lonely at the top, for that was not her experience. She attributes that to good friends in nursing who were supportive and mentioned three of those friends: Dr. Hattie Bessent, Dr. Rhetaugh Dumas, and Mrs. Barbara Nichols.

Lessons Learned

- Know thyself. Know your values.

- A personal philosophy enables you to remain anchored.

- Take pride in professional practice.

- Don't let "petty stuff" get in the way.

- Leadership is a journey. You are constantly developing and evolving.

- Good leaders are magnanimous.

- Recognize the talent of others and acknowledge it.

- No one else can steal your talent.

- Trust people. They want what you want. They also want good outcomes.

- Be about making things better on behalf of patients and their families.

GLORIA SMITH, RN, PHD, FAAN, is a distinguished leader with exceptional qualities who started out her career in nursing as a public health nurse in Detroit after completing her BSN at Wayne State University. She received her MS in nursing and an MS and PhD in anthropology from the University of Michigan. She was dean at the University of Oklahoma. From there, she became the first woman to head the State of Michigan's Department of Public Health. In 1988, Smith became the dean of Wayne State University. In 1991, she began her work and continued her strong career at the W.K. Kellogg Foundation in Battle Creek, Michigan. At the foundation, she was the vice president for programs in health. She retired in 2001. She is known for her exemplary leadership in private and public domains in the United States and abroad. The scope of her influence in nursing, healthcare, and health policy arenas transcends local, state, and national boundaries to encompass several foreign countries. Through her professional initiatives in private and public sectors, she has forged a broad perspective on the meaning, significance, and essential characteristics of care, education, and research in nursing and health service systems. Her work over a lifetime has demonstrated a commitment to improve the health and quality of life of people in underserved communities. She has "shaken up the neighborhood" throughout her career. She is known for the power of her penetrating assessments and insights in complex situations. Her international work in Africa and South America helped to increase the numbers of nurses in severely underserved regions by more than 9,000. She also left her mark at Prairie View A&M University in Texas, the only historically black college or university in Texas with a school of nursing. Smith was a founding member of the Black Nurses Association. At the W.K. Kellogg Foundation, she was the brains and soul behind the Community Partnerships Initiatives in Health professions education. These initiatives funded community-based interdisciplinary health professions education nationally with a focus on increasing access to cost-effective, culturally competent healthcare provided by nurse practitioners (NP) and NP-run faculty practices serving medically underserved communities in rural communities. Under her leadership, the foundation funded NP database efforts that continue to provide important policy-making data for the development of the graduate NP workforce. The NP curriculum and workforce data also served as the foundation that has justified moving the specialty NP masters degree to a DNP degree.

The only way you can pursue new avenues in healthcare is through collaboration
—Connie Carino, RN, DNSc, FAAN

18

DOING IT YOUR WAY: AN INTERVIEW WITH CONNIE CARINO

Written by Tine Hansen-Turton, BA, MGA, JD

In the 1950s, baccalaureate programs in nursing were not common, but Skidmore College had started one to define a new nurse with more autonomy. Connie Carino entered the program. Unlike other nursing programs that emphasized nurses as subordinates of physicians, Skidmore nursing students were shown a wider scope of what the nursing discipline could do. "You felt you had autonomy. At Skidmore we were taught that if a physician came up to a desk, you did not have to give up your chair— which was the norm in those days."

ACADEMIA ALLOWS A CAREER WOMAN FLEXIBILITY TO RAISE HER CHILDREN

After graduating from nursing school with a specialty in medical surgery, Connie received a grant from the National Institute of Mental Health to pursue her master's degree. The government was encouraging nurses to enter the psychiatric field, and Connie took advantage of those federal funds. She then taught at the University of Hawaii for a few years but returned to school for her doctorate in nursing science, with a specialty in psychiatric nursing. In between her degrees, Connie also raised a family. "Academia allows you to do family and work—it allowed me to have flexibility."

She was in her mid-40s when she launched her serious career at the University of Pennsylvania (UPenn), moving to Philadelphia when her children were older: "You have to do it your way."

EVERYONE HAS TO WIN

In the 1980s, Connie came to the UPenn to build a bridge between education and practice, to upgrade the psychiatric nursing curriculum, and to start a service where the psychiatric needs were addressed within the hospital. From her Skidmore days, she had learned that regardless of whether a system was patriarchal or matri-archal, "The only way you can pursue new avenues in healthcare is through collaboration. Everyone has to win."

She was the first doctorally prepared clinical nurse to work in the UPenn hospital. There was no link between nursing in the hospital and the nursing school at that time. The faculty of the UPenn nursing school dreamed that nursing faculty members, like their colleagues in medicine, would be allowed to practice in the hospital and get paid for it. While they were able to accomplish the first part of the goal, to have faculty members practice in both the nursing school and the hospital, reimbursement from the hospital did not follow—the nursing school had to pay the bill.

When Nursing and Medicine Collaborate, Healthcare Works Smoothly

The chair of psychiatry eventually appointed Connie to a dual faculty role at the school of medicine and the school of nursing. This was a big leap, proving Connie's ability to build bridges. In her role as a nurse in medicine, she built new psychiatric units. There was a part-nership between her and the department chair. Together, they built a model of communications up, down, and across the hospital. "When nursing and medicine collaborated things worked smoothly."

A mentor has to be tough and honest with you. Throughout her career at UPenn, Connie was fortunate enough to have Claire Fagin as a mentor. "Now and then you run into a Claire Fagin. Unfortu-nately, women often think they have to break away from anyone guiding them; they can be harder to mentor."

While she was working in her dual role, her sister was diagnosed with cancer. The death of her sister in 1985 made her look at her pro-fessional life and reevaluate it. At this point in her life, Connie was chair of psychiatric nursing in the nursing school, clinical director and director of the medical psychiatric 400-bed unit at the hospital, and manager of two budgets—one at the school of nursing and the other in the hospital. In 1987, she herself was diagnosed with cancer. "I got very fatalistic. There were no support groups." She wanted as normal a life as possible, but found there were no places offering the kind of support she, and others like her, needed.

On a trip to Italy, she read a book in which she learned about The Wellness Community (TWC) and thought that Philadelphia needed this resource, too. TWC is a national non-profit organization dedicated to providing free emotional support, education, and hope for people with cancer and their loved ones. Through participation in professionally led support groups, educational workshops, and mind/body programs utilizing the Patient Active Concept, people affected by cancer can learn vital skills to regain control of their lives, reduce feelings of isolation, and restore hope—regardless of the stage of disease.

When she came back from Italy, she traveled to Santa Monica, California, to visit TWC. She participated in a group. She talked about her illness and felt it was a powerful experience. "Professionals that get sick don't get the help they need." For the first time, she could deal with the grief over her sister's illness and death, as well as talk about her own illness and fears. She came back a renewed person and began the work toward establishing a wellness community in the Philadelphia region. Her initial thought was to establish it within the school of nursing at UPenn. But she soon realized that the establishment of TWC had to be done outside the school of nursing and academia. She approached Len Abramson, of US HealthCare, to explore funding such a community. Len, whose wife had had breast cancer, gave Connie a $75,000 seed grant. This grant gave her credibility and enabled her to raise additional funds and establish a board of directors. Beyond helping patients, she wanted a nurse to be a leader. Connie ran the center, which initially called home a basement on City Line Avenue in Philadelphia. Through her struggles to build The Wellness Center of Philadelphia, Connie found that people supported her because she was a nurse, and a nurse trying to do this lent credibility. She had done this work for 20-30 years and had a *lot* of personal credibility.

CONNIE CARINO, RN, DNSC, FAAN, is retired and currently an emeritus professor at the University of Pennsylvania. She is on the advisory board for the Independence Foundation nurse-managed health center initiatives. She is the founder of the Philadelphia Wellness Community. The Wellness Community is a national non-profit organization dedicated to providing free emotional support, education, and hope for people with cancer and their loved ones. For years, Connie was an educator and has taught at the University of Hawaii, the Catholic University, and the University of Pennsylvania. At the University of Pennsylvania, she held a joint clinical director appointment in psychiatry in both the schools of nursing and medicine. She has a BS in nursing from Skidmore College, an MS and DNC from Catholic University, and an honorary doctorate from Allegheny University. Her focus has been on the psychological and emotional response to serious medical illness.

Nursing leaders believe in the profession, keep their focus on the patient, understand the role of caring in the context of a variety of human emotions, and persevere.

—Terry Fulmer

19

THREE PRINCIPLES OF LEADERSHIP: WILLINGNESS TO COMMUNICATE, NEGOTIATE, AND COMPROMISE

Written by Terry Fulmer, RN, PhD, FAAN

The opportunity to achieve the status of "leader" in any organization is a exhilarating, sometimes daunting, moment in a career. Leadership is both perilous and fun at the same time. All of us who aspire to a leadership role are responsible to communicate ways in which other individuals who share that aspiration might benefit from lessons learned that have been important in the process. This conversation provides such an opportunity.

Karen Katen, president of Pfizer Global Pharmaceuticals, has noted that "truly effective leadership requires more than a commitment to performance—it also requires a positive attitude and a healthy balanced perspective on life" (2004, Magee, p vii). This sound commentary reminds all of us that leadership takes place within a context, and it is the ability to keep and maintain a positive context that makes those around us want to stay engaged. For the profession of nursing, there has never been a more important moment in time to keep all of us engaged in the monumental task before us. Debates regarding patient safety, cross training, shortages, the aging of our faculty, and new credentialing scenarios require that all of us exert all of our influence and leadership capacity for the benefit of the public that has put so much trust in us.

How, then, do we recognize the leaders among us? For me personally, I feel I am in the presence of a leader when my talents are maximally used, when I feel confident in those around me, and when I am asked to take responsibility for my actions. Leaders know how to extract talent from those around them, and they get the benefits from that talent because they know how to share their vision and belief system. Nursing leaders believe in the profession, keep their focus on the patient, understand the role of caring in the context of a variety of human emotions, and persevere. I especially resonate with leaders who exude honesty, fairness, kindness, and the ability to have fun while achieving important goals. Leadership is both an art and science, much the same as professional nursing is an art and science. Leaders know how to communicate effectively, develop those around them, focus on key issues, avoid micromanagement, keep a personal and professional balance, and link others for the benefit of a greater good.

I have been asked to share a case in leadership, and my example will be the historic change at the New York University (NYU) when the Division of Nursing, which was founded in 1932 as a Division of Nursing in the School of Education, was recently moved. Originally a cluster of courses in the physical education department, the division was created for those who had teaching as a career choice. In those days, if a nurse aspired to a graduate degree, it meant that her goal was to become a teacher of nursing, thus the placement within the School of Education. On February 3, 2005, David McLaughlin, provost of NYU, announced that the Division of Nursing was destined to become the College of Nursing in the College of Dentistry as of September 1, 2005. What happened to spark this momentous change?

The three principles that guided this change, in my opinion, were a willingness to communicate, a willingness to negotiate, and a willingness to compromise. Each of these principles is a theme that recurs throughout the change process that took place at NYU College of Nursing.

When I began my sojourn as head of the Division of Nursing at NYU in January 2002, I was invited to act as the interim head of the division when my predecessor stepped down precipitously due to administrative differences with the previous dean of the School of Education. The vacuum in leadership created an opportunity for me to step into an exciting role at a difficult time for the division. The horrors of September 11, 2001, were still very distinct in our memories, and our faculty members were trying to heal from that disaster as well as the recent loss of a cherished nursing leader. My role, as I saw it, was to stabilize the division and create a sense of steadiness during this turbulent time.

A national search was underway for a permanent division head. Despite warnings offered to me, I declared myself a candidate even while working as the interim head. This decision to act in an interim role is considered dangerous for a potential candidate. In an interim role, people have the opportunity to "try you on" and see characteristics they might not see during the standard—and often brief—interview process. For me, this was ideal. I loved my job as a professor of geriatric nursing at NYU and wanted more than anything to have the division stable and healthy once again. Further, I truly believed that if individuals within the division did not like me in the interim position, then they would not be supportive if I were to accept a permanent role. I was extremely secure in my faculty position, and I felt it was a position I could happily return to if I were not selected as the new division head. True, my ego would be bruised, but I would have meaningful and important work to which I could return. I had lost elections before and was able to move through those losses. I felt I could do it again.

My goal during my interim phase was to move ahead as if there was no new person coming to take my place. I wanted to proceed as if I was the permanent head, in order to create momentum for whoever would eventually take over. Further, I did not want a stranger recruited to chart our destiny in the division without a great deal of forethought. We were—and are—a group of smart, capable professionals who thrive in an environment of autonomy and individuality while pulling for the collective mission of our nursing program. This has been the history of NYU nursing. During this period of uncertainty, we all felt the need to move forward with our recruitment and retention, exams and teaching, committees, and social events. In

May 2002, we all participated in a faculty retreat to commit to what we valued and what we were looking for in the future for NYU nursing. My reasons for leading a retreat as an interim head were several, but most important was to set a baseline from which we could negotiate with a new leader if, in fact, we were to have one.

It is uncomfortable to be a candidate and interim head when others are coming in for their interviews. Colleagues are extremely polite, but everyone knows that it is unnerving to have external people competing for your job. Mercifully, the spring went by quickly as the candidates came and went. My name was among the three that were forwarded to the dean. I was selected to be the new head of the division, and a sense of heartfelt passion for NYU nursing set in. I was truly honored to be selected. Further, it was affirming to me to know that my colleagues shared this opinion. I turned to the context of the division, not just in the School of Education, but in the university.

We were in a tumultuous period of change. A new president was inducted at NYU who took us through the 9/11 grieving period. John Sexton became the 15th president of NYU in the fall of September, 2001, and by the end of 2002 it became known that the current dean of the School of Education would be stepping down. For me, this meant that I would immediately be in a position to be uncertain as to who would be my new boss. This was not a new experience. As a staff nurse, I had been on units where the head nurse resigned and an acting head nurse took over while the search was completed. I observed that this was a time of great freedom and opportunity—in times of "unfreezing," much can be accomplished. In fact, while we were acclimating to a new president, we got a new provost, a new vice president for health affairs, a new acting dean of the School of Education, and the opportunity to communicate to leaders at NYU what our profession, and our program in particular, could offer the university.

Communication within the division faculty and between faculty and the university became extremely important. A new dean would be chosen for the School of Education, and we were asked, as one of the 13 units in the school, to participate in a search for the new dean. Here was an opportunity to give voice to what could foster a thriving nursing community. We all saw this as an opportunity to recruit a leader who might be sympathetic to the idea of letting nursing become a free-standing, autonomous school as is the prevailing model in our peer nursing programs. This was not to be. The president spoke of "the enterprise university"—with fewer silos and more collectivity of thought and deed. He was not supportive of initiating new schools that were, by comparison, small and economically unknown.

In his message was a second message. How was nursing going to envision itself as an "enterprise player" at the university going forward? I began to hold additional faculty meetings to clarify what I thought I saw happening at NYU in this period of change and felt that the opportunity to redefine nursing at NYU could best take place in a new configuration. I had carefully scrutinized the 12 deans of NYU. I looked for a partner who was clinically oriented and understood what was unique to those of us responsible for patient care. The dean of medicine was not an option, given the opportunity at this point in time. To go with medicine would have been, in my mind, "retro," given the history of the profession, and such a move would do little to distinguish the opportunity before us. The new provost said that a strategic assessment committee would be formed to conduct an analysis of the School of Education while searching for a new dean.

I was invited to participate as a member of the strategic assessment process and through that process I was able to serve as a voice for NYU nursing. The charge of the provost was to review the school for the future and examine all of its component parts. All of us anticipated that the review process would take about six months and the dean search could last for two years. The exact opposite occurred. The strategic assessment committee went on for well over two years while the dean search lasted for only six months. A new dean was recruited from the Boston College Lynch School of Education and began working with us in the spring semester of 2003. As she joined, she also joined the strategic assessment committee, and the dynamics shifted dramatically from a committee that was originally determining what goals were important to adopting goals the new dean felt were important.

I continued to believe my purpose on that committee was to consider what was best for the School of Education, while giving voice to nursing and speaking to my colleagues regarding our profession and our long-standing aspiration for an independent school of nursing. In the United States, there are over 600 baccalaureate schools of nursing, and we were at a loss at NYU to understand why we could not join those ranks.

After so many years as a division, what created an environment for change? As in any complex system, universities have moments of unfreezing, and certainly the change in leadership at the School of Education, coupled with a strategic assessment process that illuminated the views of the faculty across a number of important issues, was at play. But what else happened?

The Institute of Medicine's report, *Crossing the Quality Chasm*, (2003) that mandates interdisciplinary work for the future of healthcare played an enormous role for us. The College of Nursing at NYU will be located administratively in the College of Dentistry. Dentistry? Yes, dentistry. When one thinks of the untapped opportunities in front of us in pairing these two professions, the vision takes shape. There are 300,000 dentists in the United States and 60 Colleges of dentistry. Dentists are arguably some of the most regularly visited, albeit feared, practitioners in the country. More Americans see their dentist annually than they see their physician. Therein lies the opportunity. At the NYU College of Dentistry, more than 1200 patients are seen daily. None receive a glaucoma screen. None routinely have their blood pressure taken or their urine tested for sugar and acetone. I would argue that the opportunities for nursing and dentistry are enormous. Think what might take shape in pairing these two professions with an eye on patient care outcomes?

Nurse practitioners in most states have primary care practices and prescriptive authority, and certainly in most states this is true as long as collaborative agreements are in place. With a nurse practitioner office down the hall from a dental clinic, consumers would be afforded more accessible healthcare. For frail older adults, this could make the difference between a visit or no visit. We need to be consumer-driven when thinking about how the extra decade of healthcare will be delivered. When a mother comes for a dental appointment, a pediatric nurse practitioner could be available for a well-baby visit. Many of us would long for this chance. Imagine a baby boomer generation, so utterly accustomed to the ease of one-stop-shopping! As one of them, I would welcome the opportunity to begin to bring my practitioners together.

Further, what about the shared teaching opportunities? We've been told that interdisciplinary education is not only important, but that it is essential for the future. Nurses and dentists both require strong basic science courses, physical assessment classes, ethics classes, genetics, bioterrorism, and on and on. While none of us would expect an 18-year old freshman in nursing to be in classes with a graduate dental student, our graduated students, and possibly our previously degreed students with a wealth of life experience, have much to share. One need only look at the dire state of mouth care in nursing practice to note we have much to learn. When did mouth care stop being a valued component of excellent nursing practice? And when did hospitals decide to stop providing the essential equipment nurses need to provide excellent mouth care? There is so much to be done and so much synergy in front of us.

Creating change takes courage. Some have already argued that dentistry diminishes the stature of nursing as a profession and nursing diminishes the stature of the dental profession. These arguments do little to advance our understanding of patient care outcomes that are certainly much more important as a measure of the stature of either profession.

Finally, and certainly equally if not more important, are the research opportunities. Both professions have institutes at NIH and have already proven the necessity for independence in these structures given the unique dimensions of each discipline. However, adding the other discipline to our research teams might augment the possibilities for better understanding of patient care needs and outcomes in ways not yet explored. I recognize that many nurses and dentists do research together, but it is certainly not normative. Exploring issues of pain management, ethics, genetics, comfort, and quality of life, for example, would be of great interest to both professions, and I would argue there would be parsimony in these models that would be very interesting to document. If the board of trustees at NYU had voted to make nursing a free-standing school instead of a unit within dentistry, would we be as innovative as we are now?

REFERENCES

Institute of Medicine Committee on Quality of Health Care in America. (2001). *Crossing the quality chasm*. National Academy Press. Washington, D.C.

Magee, M. (2004). *Positive leadership*. Spencer Books. Bronxville, NY.

TERRY FULMER, PhD, RN, FAAN, is The Erline Perkins McGriff Professor and dean of the College of Nursing at the College of Dentistry at New York University. She received her bachelor's degree from Skidmore College, her master's and doctoral degrees from Boston College, and her Geriatric Nurse Practitioner Post-Master's Certificate from New York University. Dr. Fulmer's program of research focuses on acute care of the elderly. Specifically, on elder abuse and neglect. She has received the status of fellow in the American Academy of Nursing, the Gerontological Society of America, and the New York Academy of Medicine. She completed a Brookdale National Fellowship and is a Distinguished Practitioner of the National Academies of Practice. Dr. Fulmer was the first nurse to be elected to the board of the American Geriatrics Society and the first nurse to serve as the president of the Gerontological Society of America.

VI

LEADERSHIP IS ... VISIONARY

Nursing engages in a life-death journey, participates in birthing-living-
suffering-playing-loving-dying as the very fabric of human existence.
The moral and visionary compass for my journey comes not from the head
but from the heart. It consists of me following the story line already laid out
from our ancestors, our visionaries from the past, but nevertheless a story line
needing to be picked up again for this postmodern time, reconstructed anew,
in order to navigate through the troubled times of the latter part of the 20th
century and now into the 21st century and a new millennium.

—Jean Watson

20

CONVERSATIONS AND REFLECTIONS ON MY JOURNEY INTO THE HEART OF NURSING: HUMAN CARING-HEALING

Written by Jean Watson, RN, PhD, FAAN

CONVERSATIONS WITH SELF AND OTHERS
RELATED TO MY JOURNEY

I ask myself, as you may ask yourself: What is this moral, visionary map which has inspired and inspirited this so-called leadership? Is it my writing, teaching, speaking, administering, living, being, becoming, evolving in my life and work in the world? What is the essence of this conversation I am having—not with you, but with myself? As I ask myself these rhetorical, philosophical questions about my life and my life work, I discover new truths about myself and my own motivations—truths and motivations which have lain dormant in my subconscious until this point in my career. These remembrances are now activated for this essay as I attempt to recapture my "Conversation" and dialogue with others at my Independence Foundation presentation.

My journey as an "identified leader" in nursing has taken me, and continues to take me, into the heart of nursing—the soul of nursing, to be more specific. That is, the spirit of nursing is why we are here. It is that timeless, essential core of nursing that embraces its very foundation, humanity itself, and acknowledges that the heart of nursing is ultimately about preserving humanity, sustaining human caring when it is threatened, and preserving human dignity—our own and others' very humanness. Nursing engages in a life-death journey, participates in birthing-living-suffering-playing-loving-dying as the very fabric of human existence. Nursing honors the deeply human-to-human connections that are life-giving-life-receiving for self-other-community-society-planet Earth-the universe.

This heart-rending focus of nursing offers energy and inspiration, the moral foundation for the discipline of nursing, transcending the passing fads and fashions of the profession at a given point in time. This essential core of nursing transcends trends in health/medical/sick care/cure/life-saving models for medical treatments, protocols, technologies. This essential core of caring, healing, and humanity provides the moral and philosophical values that are the foundation for the discipline and not only differs from but even transcends conventional nursing science and conventional nursing practices.

Human caring and healing for self and other is one of the greatest gifts we personally and professionally can offer to self and other, especially when humanity and its survival are in despair, turmoil, conflict from within and without, facing existential-spiritual-environmental crises of living/dying/changing/growing/evolving/becoming. The human dimensions of nursing are the bedrock, the moral motivation which sets the values frame that serves as the moral map/vision/guide and mentor into our future. This timeless bedrock is especially precious at this time between modern-postmodern eras, when other aspects of our lives, practices, and profession seem to have gone awry.

It is here in the light/dark places of humanity that nursing addresses, celebrates, and honors the human spirit, in which nursing lives, grows, and evolves into its maturity as a caring healing health profession. This place of maturing, this "now-space" between paradigms, centuries, and worldviews is propelled by nursing's heritage, traditions, wisdoms, and insights throughout the ages. This comes not from us, but through us today from our ancestors across time and space and national/geographic boundaries, uniting nursing as a moral, values-guided discipline and profession around the globe.

My Leadership Guide

It is this deeply human foundation of the discipline of nursing which has sustained, guided, inspired, and inspirited me to be/become—evolve—in and for nursing in my own way. Following the ancient story line of nursing and my own inner voice and vision of what

175

nursing is, and yet has not actualized for itself or for society, is what has motivated and energized my work and career. Through circumstances in which I found myself with various career options, I have sought to bring forth a voice of hope and action where appropriate and possible.

From where I happened to be, in different positions, at different points in time, I have pursued an opening up of the human spirit and creativity, appealing to our human heart and the heart of nursing, holding a vision of new possibilities where others have often been discouraged, dispirited, or detoured from the bigger vision.

It is easy to be pulled toward conformity or the status quo to "fit in" or to be "normal" and to gain "acceptance" within the dominant framework. Thus nursing often has pursued conforming to what is, or catching up with the dominant paradigm, rather than sustaining its timeless dimensions and envisioning what might be within its own foundation and moral map running through time as a timeless gift for humanity itself. However, we are in a time and space between our evolution and awakening in which we still need to learn about ourselves and our own power *with*, not *over*, another person, another nation, another culture, another nationality, another's values and subjective life reality for their own humanity. And on it goes.

At this point, we can and must hold an inspired vision for nursing and humanity's survival into this new millennium. We have reached a new era in human history. Nursing in its maturing role, adhering to its disciplinary foundation and values, can and is helping to craft a new world order and moral community. When caring, healing, wholeness, connectedness, and compassionate human service manifest the evolving human spirit and infinite field of creativity and visionary moral ideals for humanity, we are contributing to the healing of self, other, society, the planet Earth, and the very universe.

How lofty these ideas and ideals, but simultaneously how true and how inspiring as a basis for sustaining nursing and honoring this ancient and noble profession for its survival across time and space. So, in being asked to write about or offer a "conversation" about my journey of leadership in nursing, I digress to the most primal, basic foundation of my motivation and strength. Thus the moral and visionary compass for my journey comes not from the head but from the heart. It consists of me following the story line already laid out from our ancestors, our visionaries from the past, but nevertheless a story line needing to be picked up again for this postmodern time, reconstructed anew, in order to navigate through the troubled times of the latter part of the 20th century and now into the 21st century and a new millennium.

I believe we are creating a revised story line to remind us how to navigate into and through the 21st century, when everything we knew, worked for, and tried to accomplish with a narrowly defined medical techno-science focus is dissolving before our very eyes, as we move through time and space. This is the time and space that Martha Rogers intuited with her prescience whereby the non-physical reality becomes more real than the physical, whereby energy is the metaphor for healing and treatments, and human spirit and the energetic consciousness of caring and connectedness reunite us and nursing across time and geographic boundaries into a new era in human health and healing traditions and practices.

HIGHLIGHTS AND EXEMPLARS OF ACTIONS WHICH AFFECTED NURSING AND GUIDED MY DECISIONS AND LEADERSHIP ACTIONS

Writing—Treatise on nursing as the philosophy and science of caring became the origin of all other acts, in that in attempting to more fully actualize the Nightingale vision of nursing, my first work led me toward greater depths of scholarship, teaching, more writing, research, increasing roles and responsibilities, and various positions. These positions have ranged from and included department head, academic associate dean to school of nursing dean, to distinguished professor, visiting professorships, Kellogg and Fulbright awards, to invited keynotes around the nation and world. More recently, I am consulting on, teaching, and implementing the model of caring-healing in a variety of ways as a professional practice guide and as a curricular-pedagogical guide, having it serve as a deeper level of personal-professional practice in making *Caritas Connections* between caring-love-healing-peace in my personal life and work.

Creation of Center for Human Caring—The Center for Human Caring (CHC), which was created with my guidance and vision at University of Colorado School of Nursing in the 1980s, became a source of creative change, transformative educational-pedagogical thinking for a caring curriculum, as well as an interdisciplinary, intellectual and clinical demonstration project for experimenting with caring theory-guided practice models. It was a source of innovation for critiquing and developing caring science knowledge and its intersection with philosophy, ethics, arts and humanities, and new forms of healing practices for nursing education and healthcare practices. As such it served somewhat as a research and development center for ontologically and empirically validating and affirming caring philosophy and ethics within a caring science context for education, practice, and research. The center served as a symbol and exemplar for nursing and nurses around the world and as a site where scholars and practitioners visited and learned during its decade of activities and continuing programs. (For more information on continuing programs that emerged from the original Center for Human Caring, including the International Certificate in Caring-Healing program, go to www.uchsc.edu/nursing/caring.)

Creation of new level advanced nursing practice of caring-healing—During another period of acute national nursing shortage in the mid-to-late 1980s, our public university school envisioned nursing for the 21st century when the school would be 100 years old. As dean of nursing at the time, collaborative and creative intellectual and financial partnerships were created between the school and clinical agencies as well as private foundations, even in the midst of those who were skeptical. Thus, against tremendous odds, and often limited support, partnerships were formed and collaborative relationships within and without resulted in the University of Colorado developing a career professional clinical doctorate program (nursing doctor), the first public-supported university in the United States to do so. The formal planning and implementing of the program allowed for a decade of change—moving from the vision to the awarding of the degree, with formal collaborative partners in the community and state. This program laid the foundation for what is the latest national movement toward a unified clinical practice doctorate (DNP). While the DNP is soon to be the national, standard degree for advanced practice nursing, the ND (nursing doctorate) program was unique in that it built upon the history of the nurse practitioner program at the University of Colorado but emphasized a mature *nursing qua nursing* disciplinary focus on caring-healing-health-wholeness and new advanced modalities and practice roles and creative possibilities, in and out of conventional institutions and settings.

MORE RECENTLY . . .

Creation of new professional caring-theory-guided practice models and caring-healing nursing units (Attending Caring Nursing

Model™ of practice and research and Nightingale Units™ are examples)—With the current crisis of nursing shortage, retention and advancement of clinical nursing—along with more recent incentives for hospitals to achieve Magnet recognition—increasing numbers of hospitals and clinical agencies are introducing caring philosophies and caring theory. This effort seems to serve as one of the criteria to restore, retain, and encourage advancement of nurses and nursing. There is a parallel phenomenon in nursing education, with the rise of advanced practice, with attention to holistic caring and healing, and a desire for new forms of curricula and pedagogies.

Thus, my recent scholarship has expanded to more formally include caring-theory-guided activities and educational-practice directions within the caring model. The clinical activities range from using caring theory as a philosophical-ethical guide to restore the heart of nursing practices, to more formal use of "carative factors" as a middle range theory format, including use of caring theory language and documentation systems. Other initiatives include creating "Nightingale units" as caring-healing units, including healing environments for nurses and patients and families alike. As the practices expand, I am working on developing "caritas coaches" so that others can pass on the culture, knowledge, and skills related to authentic caring/living the theory in practice situations and personal life. Other examples include cultivating "Attending Caring Nursing Model™ /Attending Caring Team Model" as demonstrations of advanced professional practice, taking responsibility for "attending to whole person/family, caring-healing needs," going beyond medical-treatment/ system responsibilities, making oneself directly accountable to patient for care and providing system leadership for new standards of care.

Caritas nursing models and practices—Creating forums in teaching and practice worlds that are uniting personal practice of caring and healing with deep personal work, at ontological-ethical level. This work consists of cultivating a deeply authentic caring-healing practice referred to as *caritas*, which integrates caring and a deep source of love, helping self and others to engage and commit to creating/ becoming the caritas field, which is the tipping point for transforming self and system.

This caritas field work is now being generated privately and publicly in educational and clinical settings around the globe wherever others are inclined to engage at this deep level of self practice. This is an invitation and skill I am cultivating wherever I am speaking, consulting, or practicing. The goal is to create a new way of being human; becoming the caritas that one wishes to have in one's own life. Thus others are invited to join in a global agenda of uniting one's personal practice with professional practice, knowing the personal is the professional. It is the nurse's consciousness, intentionality, and energetic field-pattern of caring and love which becomes the transformative source for change.

Passing the light of nursing around the world—Since the 1990s, I have been inviting nurses around the world to re-create meaningful rituals in their work and world. This is done through the symbolic passing on of the light of nursing with a candlelight ritual. This act is conducted, literally and metaphorically, during formal presentations and papers around the world. The practice is enacted by using a candle that has been around the world of nurses at least 10 times now, lighting a new candle from the original light, first begun in 1992. The new candle, lit energetically and literally by the light of the first candle which initiated the ritual, stays with the audience in which it is delivered and the new group, individually and collectively decides how to use the candle to keep the ritual alive and continue to pass on the light of nursing, a symbolic and power-filled act that reconnects nursing through time and space with the original light image of Nightingale. This simple act helps to restore the heart and soul of nursing and nurses as they reconnect with their light source. It is reported to be a healing act helping nurses to remember why they are nurses.

REFERENCES

Foster, R. (2003). Research: The attending caring nurse project. *Caring for our future*. The Children's Hospital Association. Denver, CO.

Quinn, J. (1992). Holding sacred space: The nurse as healing environment. *Holistic Nursing Practice*. 6(4):26-35.

Quinn, J. (2003). Revisioning the nursing shortage: A call to caring for healing the healthcare system. *Frontiers of Health Care Management*. 19(2):3-21.

Stuller, S. (2004) Evolution of the attending caring nurse model. *Caring for our future*. The Children's Hospital Association. Denver, CO.

Watson, J. (2005). *Caring science as sacred science*. Philadelphia: FA Davis.

Watson, J. (2003). Love and caring: Ethics of face and hand. *Nursing Administrative Quarterly*. 27(3):197-202

Watson, J. (2002). Intentionality and caring-healing consciousness: A practice of transpersonal caring. *Holistic Nursing Practice*.16 (4):1-8.

Watson, J. (1999). *Postmodern nursing and beyond*. New York: Elsevier.

Watson, J. & Foster, R. (2003). The attending caring nursing model. *Journal of Clinical Nursing*. 12, 360-365.

Woodward, T. (2004). Attending caring nurse model: Part II: Caring praxis. *Caring for our future*. The Children's Hospital Association. Denver, CO.

JEAN WATSON, RN, PhD, FAAN, is Distinguished Professor of Nursing and holds an endowed chair in Caring Science at the University of Colorado Health Sciences Center. She is founder of the original Center for Human Caring in Colorado and is a Fellow of the American Academy of Nursing. She previously served as dean of Nursing at the University of Colorado Health Sciences Center and is a past president of the National League for Nursing. Watson earned undergraduate and graduate degrees in nursing and psychiatric-mental health nursing and holds her PhD in educational psychology and counseling. She is a widely published author and recipient of several awards and honors, including an international Kellogg Fellowship in Australia, a Fulbright Research Award in Sweden and six honorary doctoral degrees, including 3 international honorary doctorates (Sweden, United Kingdom, and Canada). She has been a distinguished lecturer and held endowed lecturer status at universities throughout the United States and many foreign countries. Her international nursing experiences have taken her around the globe several times. While director of the Center for Human Caring, she established international connections with colleague and systems in several countries, including United Kingdom, Canada, New Zealand, Australia, Scandinavia, Brazil, Thailand, Venezuela, Japan, and Korea, among others. Her published works on the philosophy and theory of human caring and the art and science of caring in nursing are used in academic programs throughout the world. Her caring philosophy is used to guide new models of caring and healing practices in diverse settings worldwide. Watson has been featured in numerous national videos on nursing theory and the art of nursing. She was the 1993 recipient of the National League for Nursing Martha E. Rogers Award which recognizes a nurse scholar who has made significant contributions to nursing knowledge that advances the science of caring in nursing and health sciences. New York University recognized her as a distinguished nurse scholar. In 1999, the Fetzer Institute honored her with the national Norman Cousins Award in recognition of her commitment to developing; maintaining, and exemplifying relationship-centered care practices.

It is no wonder nurses have been described
as exhibiting "oppressed group" behavior because so many of us have been socialized
to think that we have to be twice as good
to be any good.
—Angela Barron McBride

21

LEADERSHIP:
REFLECTIONS OF A FEMINIST

Written by Angela Barron McBride, RN, PhD, FAAN

I grew up conventionally in the 1940s and 1950s. My father earned the family income and my mother did just about everything else—from cleaning and cooking to helping with homework and smoothing over family tensions. I wanted to go to college, because that was my mother's dream, both for herself and for me, and I knew from early on that education was the one socially acceptable way for me to be able to leave home; otherwise, you lived at home until you married.

I often joke that I grew up in a world where the only career options open to girls were becoming a teacher, a nurse, or a nun, in which case you became either a teacher or a nurse. Having worked all through high school as a nurse's aide—doing all sorts of things that one would never now be allowed to do as an untrained teenager, from gavage-feeding premature infants to carrying a stillborn baby to the morgue—I headed off to Georgetown University School of Nursing. At the time, Georgetown required all applicants to take an admission test that had to be individually arranged, and mine was scheduled on a Saturday at my high school. One of the nuns on the faculty had graciously agreed to proctor the examination on her day off. There was a blizzard that day that caused public transportation to come to a halt, so I walked about five miles roundtrip, accompanied by my father, to take the exam, which did result in a four-year presidential scholarship. I think that was the first time in my life I really thought that my going to nursing school was somehow preordained!

Was I leader early on? Yes. I was active in school and community affairs, editing our high school literary magazine and becoming the first girl to become president of our parish chapter of the Catholic Youth Organization. In college, I became the first woman officer of Georgetown's theatre group, The Mask & Bauble. I don't know that I really saw myself as a leader. I was seen that way, though I was more inclined to think, "If I am their leader, then they really are in trouble!"

My sense of self changed when I started graduate work at Yale in 1962. Afterward, I stayed on to teach at Yale. This was the first time in my life that I met a number of women—Lucy Conant, Donna Diers, Rhetaugh Dumas, Nancy French, Virginia Henderson, Jean Johnson, Rachel Robinson, Liz Sharp, Florence Wald, Ernestine Wiedenbach—who took their work seriously—even if they did not take themselves too seriously. This was also the time when I first read Simone de Beauvoir's *The Second Sex* and Betty Friedan's *The Feminine Mystique*, both of which were major consciousness-raising experiences. Up until that time, I had tended to believe what I read. Sure, I knew that points of view were shaped by culture and the times, but it was only after reading those books that I began to question my basic assumptions about how reality was constructed. I was particularly affected in my thinking by de Beauvoir's role distinction between *immanence* (women are typically assigned by society to maintenance work) and *transcendence* (men are expected to do the things that shape society and address the future). I knew then that I wanted a little transcendence in my life!

I became a mother in 1967, and I was particularly open to new thoughts about motherhood. Old notions—he's the head and she's the heart of the family—gave way to new convictions that every family needed parents with one of each (head and heart) so children could combine the two in their lives. When our second daughter was born in 1970, I started writing my thoughts and feelings down thinking I would share them with my children some day (sort of my way of explaining myself). These reflections eventually became *The Growth and Development of Mothers*, which became the first critically acclaimed book to analyze motherhood in light of the women's movement. Selected by both *The New York Times* and the *American Journal of Nursing* as one of the best books of 1973, this success gave me confidence in one of the areas I have come to see as very important in the development of leadership—that is, taking your own experience seriously as a lens through which to analyze what may be the generic issues of the day. Instead of taking as gospel what you read or what authorities tell you, you are willing to reflect on your experience, looking for insights into understanding the phenomenon under study.

The next decade was a busy one for me—completing a doctorate in developmental psychology, authoring a second book (*Living with Contradictions: A Married Feminist*, 1976), and taking a faculty position at Indiana University School of Nursing. I was fortunate to be named a National Kellogg Fellow (1981-84). This was a program meant to develop leadership in young professionals under the age of 40. I squeaked in the year I was to turn 40, and then lobbied successfully to change the rules because they were unfair to women who tended to not experience lockstep development in their careers. While almost all of us in this program who entered our careers in the counter-culture 1960s were reluctant to own up to being leaders, this was the turning point in my own development as a leader.

Over the course of the fellowship, I gave more and more thought to what it meant to have a full career. Eventually, I worked out a five-stage model that began with **Preparation,** then moved on to the stage of **Independent Contributions**—a move from being a novice to becoming competent. By the third stage, called **Program Development,** the focus was less on abilities, though expertise continued to be developed, and more on the development of others and of the home setting. In the fourth stage, **Development of the Field,** the professional is beginning to be seen as an authority with the purview extending beyond the home setting into shaping the profession and healthcare. The fifth stage, **The Gadfly Period,** was reserved for those who were no longer constrained by institutional identities but still involved in the field—this was the stage when one became a coach to the leaders of the field.

Without elaborating at length on this schema, this model of career development enabled me to understand that leadership really wasn't a choice if one wished to have a full career. Becoming competent or achieving expert status wasn't enough if one didn't use one's authority to shape the home setting, nurture future generations, and move forward both the profession and healthcare. These insights may not sound particularly revolutionary when I share them today, but they changed me in a profound way. I was no longer unwilling to be a leader, so when I was asked to run for president of Sigma Theta Tau International, then later for president of the American Academy of Nursing, I agreed to do so. By the time I was exerting leadership in these positions, I also understood that one should not seek to imitate excellence in others, but instead think through what one uniquely brings to such organizations. Since I was a career woman juggling work and family just like the majority of Sigma Theta Tau members, I made career and role juggling a central focus of the programming that I organized. Since I was concerned about the extent to which younger fellows in the academy did not know much about the achievements of their elders, I worked to establish the "Living Legend" program which honors those who are leaders in a group of leaders.

It was also in the late 1980s and 1990s that I became more involved in multidisciplinary groups, serving on the National Advisory Mental Health Council of the National Institutes of Mental Health (NIMH) and on the advisory board of the National Institutes of Health's Office of Research in Women's Health, and becoming dean of an eight-campus school of nursing. These experiences taught me new political skills such as language choices depending upon the audience and need. I learned, for example, how not to talk about the importance of "nursing research" but instead to talk in terms of the need for "behavioral research" in order to achieve the same goal, since only nurses care deeply about the former but many others care about the latter (nurses, psychologists, social workers, sociologists, consumers). These experiences made me realize all the more how much nursing can contribute to society's larger agendas, and I became skilled at describing what nursing can contribute to meeting either the needs of patients in a quickly changing healthcare environment or the goals of the university in an increasingly entrepreneurial world.

The early leadership literature was dominated by a preoccupation with relations-oriented and task-oriented behaviors: Does the leader demonstrate caring and integrity? Does the leader clarify tasks to be performed and monitor progress? Now there is increasing emphasis on a third aspect of leadership, the way leaders encourage organizational innovation and help others to manage change. While there are enduring values and goals—e.g., facilitating quality care that is affordable and accessible—the way that these values and goals will shape processes is constantly in flux, because the evidence base supporting best practices is constantly developing and the availability of resources is not a constant. Leadership, as it is now taking shape, is not solely defined by personal competence or expertise, but shaped instead by whether the individual can get others to work together to achieve the preferred future. Moving in this direction involves being empowered ourselves, empowering others, and creating empowering organizations.

EMPOWERING NURSES

The major task of adulthood is learning to marry concern for self with concern for others. Not coincidentally, one philosopher described a career as a mechanism for both self-development and meeting the needs of society. Nurses have long felt that push to meet the needs of others, but haven't always been reinforced to develop themselves. The "handmaiden" image of nurses has had a chilling effect on our ability to exert leadership. Since most nurses are salaried employees of institutions, they may not be encouraged to give voice to their own opinions or expectations. It is no wonder nurses have been described as exhibiting "oppressed group" behavior because so many of us have been socialized to think that we have to be twice as good to be any good. And that form of being hard on ourselves so often leads us to be unnecessarily hard then on our colleagues.

HERE IS MY LIST OF THE EMPOWERED PERSON'S CHARACTERISTICS:

- Has a sense of her own worth and that of her profession.

- Understands her personal strengths and limitations, as well as those of her profession, and acts within those terms to build on the assets and not be tripped up by the limitations.

- Networks within and outside the home setting to extend contacts and horizons.

- Recognizes and uses her or his own positional authority (stemming from office) and expert authority (stemming from knowledge base).

- Perceives self as generally effective and able to deal with change and frustration.

- Able to access and mobilize support, opportunities, and resources.

- Understands one can be effective without being perfect.

- Thinks and acts as if she or he can make a difference

- Does not make the same mistake three times in a row without rethinking assumptions and strategies.

For me, empowerment begins with having a strong sense of what you can do. It extends with not letting others define your work as merely derivative—either handmaiden or being a physician substitute. I believe that a strong sense of self and of your chosen field can be shored up by the following:

- Treating self as an "executive" who deserves to be well maintained, thus attending to the self-care strategies (sleep, relaxation, nutrition, exercise, stress management) that we regularly teach others but tend to ignore in ourselves.

- Becoming an "educated person" who is broadly knowledgeable about world events and new developments, with validated competencies in defined areas.

- Learning to network, particularly through professional organizations, so your expertise is multiplied by the abilities of colleagues and the available infrastructure supports (e.g., newsletters, list serves, journals, grant programs).

- Monitoring your thinking processes so you do not dismiss the positive, ignore the neutral, and only ruminate on the negative.

- Practicing the art of reframing—"A *no* can be useful in the next round of negotiations"; "I'm so grown up, I cannot tell the difference between failure and life experience"; "If I'm feeling depressed, it may mean that I am particularly bright, thus more disturbed by the discrepancy between what is and what could be."

- Remembering that there is a difference between knowing what to do and getting it done and that you may be so preoccupied with the former that you're not attending to the politics of the latter.

- Acting as if your opinions make a difference, even when no one invites your opinion.

I would like to elaborate on the last item because it has served me well over the years. When I was a department chair, I wrote the new dean of medicine telling him how pleased my department was with his appointment. I'm not sure that he would have recognized me even in a small group, but I wrote him "as if" the good opinion of me and my colleagues mattered to him. Judging by the warmth of the letter back to me, I think it did, even if it did not matter to him originally. A few years later, I was dean of nursing, and we enjoyed a mutually respectful relationship that had its roots, I believe, in that first encounter.

Perhaps a more profound example of this approach took place three years after our hospital consolidation. Bringing two medical cultures together had been difficult, so administration canvassed physicians for their evaluation of progress to date. Without being asked, the executive vice president for patient and nursing services and I acted "as if" we had been canvassed for our opinions, too. We wrote a three-page letter describing our considerable progress to date, highlighting unresolved problems, and ending with a recommendation that the institution move to acquire "magnet hospital" status. The letter was on the agenda of the executive committee, but time ran out twice before it could be considered. The matters raised were eventually addressed "off line," and a number of positive changes resulted. The executive vice president for patient and nursing services retired not too long thereafter, and all applicants were asked their opinion about acquiring "magnet hospital" status, which has since come to pass.

A similar strategy is pretending to be the most effective person you know when you personally feel paralyzed to change the situation at hand. A psychology colleague at a very prestigious university once took over responsibilities for a major grant after the unexpected death of her senior colleague whose name was Marcia. My friend had just completed her doctorate and felt inadequate to the task at hand, but regularly she would ask herself "What would Marcia do in this situation?" and she always had an answer even when she wasn't sure what she would do. I've adopted this strategy successfully and have regularly asked myself, "What would a good dean do in this situation?" and always came up with ideas, even though I did not know initially what I wanted to do as dean.

Empowering individuals isn't enough. We must develop organizational structures that empower individuals such as the following:

- Incorporating nurses into all aspects of the organizational structure.

- Supporting career ladders, professional practice, and self-governance.

- Engaging nurses in strategic planning, not just in maintenance activities.

- Subsidizing educational mobility (RN-BSN, RN-MSN, BSN-PhD, MSN-PhD) and developmental opportunities for all.

- Recognizing and celebrating a range of achievements with honors and newspaper stories so what nurses do is visible and they can be perceived as accomplished.

- Building mentoring structures in support of the inexperienced teacher, new researcher, and novice clinician.

- Decorating the institution with a view to nursing's heritage (e.g., photographs of nurses in action).

- Encouraging strong links between nursing service and nursing education (separately the heads of nursing service and education do not have the same power as their physician counterparts, but together they can be formidable in moving their shared agenda forward).

Being a feminist, defined by me as a person concerned both with personal development *and* the welfare of others (family, colleagues, patients, etc.), has energized me in many ways, from imagining new career possibilities for myself and developing mentoring structures for the next generation, to changing how my university saw the school of nursing and how our hospital network valued nurses. Wearing that feminist label, I would like to think that I have addressed *yin* and *yang* simultaneously, drawing attention to both the importance of nursing's invaluable maintenance work and nursing's role in exerting the transformational leadership required for healthcare to achieve its preferred future.

ANGELA BARRON MCBRIDE, RN, PhD, FAAN, is distinguished professor and university dean emerita of Indiana University School of Nursing. She has received the following degrees throughout her distinguished career: DHL (honoris causa), Purdue University, 1998; DHL (honoris causa), University of Akron, 1997; DS (honoris causa), Medical College of Ohio, 1995; DHL (honoris causa), Georgetown University, 1993; LLD (honoris causa), Eastern Kentucky University, 1991; DPS (honoris causa), University of Cincinnati, 1983; PhD, Purdue University, 1978; MSN, Yale University, 1964; BSN, Georgetown University, 1962. Her scholarly interests include the experience of parents, health concerns of women, and leadership development. Dr. McBride is author of *The Growth and Development of Mothers* (1973); *Living with Contradictions: A Married Feminist* (1976); *How to Enjoy a Good Life with your Teenager* (1987), and has more than 200 other publications to her credit. Along with Joan Austin, she compiled *Psychiatric-Mental Health Nursing: Integrating the Behavioral and Biological Sciences*, which won a 1996 *American Journal of Nursing* book-of-the-year award. An American Nurses' Foundation Scholar, she is a Kellogg Fellow, a fellow of the American Academy of Nursing, and a fellow of the American Psychological Association. McBride received the 1983 American Nurses Association Council of Specialists in Psychiatric and Mental Health Nursing Award for Current Impact in Research and Scholarship. She received the Distinguished Research Award of the Midwest Nursing Research Society in 1985 and was elected to the National Academies of Practice as a distinguished practitioner in 1986. In 1995, she was honored for her contributions to nursing and health psychology by the American Psychological Association's Division 38 and was elected to membership in the Institute of Medicine, The National Academies. She is past president of Sigma Theta Tau International (1987-89) and the American Academy of Nursing (1993-95). Currently, she serves on the Clarian Board and chairs their Quality and Patient Care Committee.

Our role should be in setting the stage and then getting out of our way so that success can happen.
—Patricia D. Wellenbach

22

TRANSITION AND SUCCESSION: EMPOWERING YOURSELF IN THE ART OF LETTING GO

Written by Patricia D. Wellenbach

When I was a nursing student in the 1970s, I vividly recall my psychology professor instructing us that the first thing you do when you enter a therapeutic relationship with a patient is plan your exit from that relationship. At the time it seemed a frivolous statement: How could that be? Figuring out how you are going to leave something when it had not even started yet?

Many years and three careers later, I know this is sage advice for anyone in a leadership position, most particularly nurses. Why is it we, as nurses, do not carry this advice with us throughout our professional lives? Candidly, we have a habit of convincing ourselves that we have to do it all, that there is not anyone who could do our work better or heaven forbid, differently, and achieve success. The reality is we are all replaceable. As scary as that might be to accept, it is really true.

I can tell you that it was in the transition, when I left my job as executive director of a nonprofit organization, that I came to understand the importance of my role. I always had a sense that the true test to my leadership would come after I had left when my staff, my board, and others would have to figure what and who came next. In order for that to happen, I had to ask myself some tough questions. Had I put in place the key ingredients that would enable the organization to recruit a visionary next leader? And if I had, could I live with the fact that the next leader might do more important things for the organization and realize new levels of achievement, things that I might not even have the capacity to do, much less make happen?

In Rachael Remen's book, *My Grandfather's Blessings,* she tells the story of the starfish. In this story, an old man is walking along the beach at low tide, and he is picking up starfish that are drying in the sun and throwing them back into the ocean. He has been doing this for a while when a jogger approaches him and asks what he is doing. The old man explains that the starfish will die in the sun and so he is throwing them back into the ocean. The younger man begins to laugh, "You are wasting your time. Can't you see that there are hundreds of starfish on this beach? Thousands of beaches in the world? And another low tide tomorrow? What makes you think you can make a difference?" With that he continues his run along the beach. The old man watches the jogger and then resumes his walk. Picking up another starfish, he tosses it back into the ocean and says: "Made a difference to that one."

I share this story with you not to illustrate the importance of one person making a difference one small action at a time, although that is an important message. There will always be thousands of "starfish" that need our help. This story reminds me that we have a responsibility to empower our organizations so others can step into our role and carry on the work: not "our" work, but "the" work. Our charge as leaders is to put systems, structures and organizational dynamics in place so that tomorrow, and the tomorrow after that, the next leaders have an opportunity to emerge. Many times organizations are not able to groom new leaders from within. Financials and human resources are not always available for that type of succession planning. What we need to do is position our organizations so that competent professionals can be brought on board ready to take the lead and bring the organizations we work with to a new level. Critical to this is being a leader who is willing to let go, willing to take your ego out of it and willing to admit that someone else can do things differently and maybe even better than you. I promise you if you can get to that mindset, the rewards are unimaginable—both for you and for your organizations. We have the capacity to help the process along and be an active participant in preparing the way for those who come after us. Our role should be in setting the stage and then getting out of our way so that success can happen.

From 1998-2005, I had the best job in the world. As the executive director of The Wellness Community of Philadelphia (TWCP), I worked with a staff whose commitment to excellence in providing support, education, and hope to people with cancer and their loved ones was extraordinary. I had an engaged working board of directors who were true partners in realizing the vision for the organization. I helped to grow the organization from an annual budget of $350,000 to $1.3 million, took the full-time staff from four to 12, participated in the creation and launch of four national educational initiatives, and successfully helped create a model program to provide services to those living with cancer in underserved communities. The organization was humming along (although not without the occasional misstep), I was at the top of my game professionally, I was recognized as an influential leader in the region for my work in the nonprofit sector, and I knew it was time to go.

When I announced my decision to step down in the fall of 2004, people were shocked. I heard so many of the expected responses. Wellness needs you too much, what will they do without you? Why now when you have so much more to offer? You are doing such a great job, why would you want to leave? I listened to all of the pleas to stay, but my inner voice told me there was no better time to go. I had worked hard with the staff and board to bring the organization to a position of strength. When I interviewed for the job, I had told the search committee that I thought it would take three to five years for me to achieve what I thought I could for the organization. We did get a bit off plan for about 18 months when I held two positions, as the executive director in Philadelphia and as the vice president of corporate and community relations for the national Wellness

Community. It was a great opportunity for us locally, for the organization nationally, and for me professionally. So some of what we had thought we would accomplish got delayed a year or so, but we eventually achieved our plan.

The board had experienced a change in leadership, and I could see new leaders emerging. The staff had taken ownership of driving initiatives and setting achievable program and organizational goals. In 2005, TWCP would begin another strategic planning process. In all reality, I knew that I would not stay for three more years to see that plan created and successfully executed. I needed to step down, let the organization begin a search for a new director from a position of strength and set a new strategic plan in place. This would be the biggest test of my leadership. Could I let go? Was my board and staff ready to accept this challenge?

Two years later as I reflect on these questions, I can say the experience of leaving was instrumental in my continued opinion that I had the best job in the world. In setting the stage, the board, staff leadership, and I worked closely to engage the organizations' various constituencies in becoming comfortable with the transition. We worked collaboratively to get the messaging right, to set and stick to a timeline and honor the process. I was involved in the announcement and had the chance to talk privately to a few key stakeholders. I helped the search committee set a list of core competencies and educated them on a more detailed understanding of the real job of the executive director. I helped to select the search firm, and then I did the most important thing of all: I got out of their way and let them do the work. I was adamant about not retaining a seat on the board. The new leadership deserved the opportunity to create their vision. Quite honestly, they needed to be able to throw me under the bus anytime and not worry about offending me or getting my permission to institute change!

So how does the story end? TWCP hired a new executive director a few months after I left. They survived a short time without the position filled and did just fine. The new executive director has her own style of leadership and a vision for the organization. My guess is that there may have been some challenges, but that is not my problem. There are talented professionals at the staff and board level that can handle whatever comes their way. Anyway, from my perspective they seem to be doing just fine. The success of TWCP was never really about me or any one individual. The success is about the work and, ultimately, about mission.

And me? Well, in all honesty the first few days and weeks were a bit strange. However, I quickly found myself again—separate from my title of *"executive director."* It was liberating in a way not to carry the responsibility. I had never really acknowledged how much an impact that responsibility had in my everyday life. After a while, I had the opportunity to do some interesting consulting work with nonprofits. I found I could share lessons learned and best practices and make a difference for other organizations. I was recruited for some board positions and discovered my years of working with my own board made me a better board member for those organizations. I eventually landed a job in the private sector. That is a whole separate story! Do I miss my colleagues at TWCP? I must honestly say "yes." Do I regret leaving? Not for one minute as my leaving was important for me *and* for the organization.

WHAT I KNOW FOR SURE

- I know that what I learned from my psychology nursing instructor is really true—start crafting your exit strategy almost as soon as you start your new job.

- Change is good, and spending time as a change agent for yourself and the place where you work can be a very rewarding experience.

- Make peace with the fact that someone can come after you and do amazing work, not necessarily in the way in which you would approach it, but it has value just the same.

- Stay true to yourself, listen to your inner voice, and take your ego out of the process—it will be very liberating.

- Hold your integrity as a touchstone—it will be the rock that supports you as you occasionally wonder, "did I make the right decision?"

Remen's book tells another story of a medical colleague of hers describing the experience of staying true to himself and equating his life to an orchestra. In times of confusion and self doubt, when he needed to reclaim his integrity, he thought of the concertmaster who, in the moments before the concert begins, asks the oboist to sound an A. He goes on to say that at first there is chaos and noise as all parts of the orchestra try to align themselves with the note. But, as the instruments begin to hit that note, the noise abates. When all the instruments come together as one, there is a moment of rest, of homecoming. He goes on to say that he is always tuning his orchestra so that deep inside him there is a sound that is his alone. Sometimes there are people and situations that help him hear his note more clearly; other times people and situations make it harder for him to hear.

When you make the decision to leave, you will hear a great deal of chaos and noise as different constituencies try to dissuade you from your decision. It will make it harder to hear your inner voice. Eventually those constituencies will come around and accept your decision. If you stay true to your inner voice, your partners in making your organization run will align, and then together you can orchestrate the transition. Being authentic and your integrity are so important in this process. Transition and succession is something you should embrace. These experiences can provide some of the most rewarding moments of your professional career.

So, what are you waiting for?

REFERENCES

Remen, R. (2001). *My Grandfather's Blessings*. Riverhead Books/ Penguin Putnam. NY.

PATRICIA D. WELLENBACH is managing director of business development and strategic initiatives with Granary Associates. She possesses extensive experience in the health care and nonprofit sectors in the areas of organizational dynamics, business development, governance and strategic planning. Her professional experience includes serving as the executive director of The Wellness Community (Philadelphia), staff development coordinator of obstetrics at Pennsylvania Hospital, and as a staff nurse. She currently serves on the boards of Abington Memorial Hospital Foundation and the Pennsylvania Academy of the Fine Arts. She also serves onthe Breast Cancer Advisory Committee of Thomas Jefferson Memorial Hospital. She is a recipient of the Benjamin Rush Award presented by the Philadelphia County Medical Society recognizing lay persons that have made outstanding contributions to the health and welfare of people in the United States. She received a BS in nursing from Boston College and completed the UCLA Health Care Executive Program.

AFTERWORD

This book came into being as a result of conversations between Tine Hansen-Turton, Vernice Ferguson, and Susan Sherman regarding the richness of the "Conversation With . . ." presentations jointly sponsored by the Independence Foundation and the National Nursing Centers Consortium. The informative and educational value of these "conversations" was strong, with much of the commentary remarkable in its clarity and depth. To lose these conversations, we knew, would have been a disservice to the healthcare industry and to leadership in general.

Most of the audience for the "Conversations With . . ." were nurses, many of whom provide healthcare services in nurse-managed health centers. The leadership these nurses provide in community clinics and centers is truly remarkable. Few people, however, are aware of their work, including politicians, policy-makers, and others. It is our hope that this book will assist in positioning these nurses—and all nurses—and their work more visibly in the public eye.

We hope this book speaks directly to you as a professional. Whether you are at the beginning, the middle, or the end of your journey, we hope you identified with much of what is written here and that the *conversations* engaged and activated you.

Tine Hansen-Turton, BA, MGA, JD

Vernice Ferguson, RN, MA, FAAN, FRCN

Susan Sherman, RN, MA